The Cold War

Bassim Hamadeh, CEO and Publisher
Angela Schultz, Senior Acquisitions Editor
Michelle Piehl, Senior Project Editor
Berenice Quirino, Associate Production Editor
Miguel Macias, Senior Graphic Designer
Stephanie Kohl, Licensing Associate
Gustavo Youngberg, Interior Designer
Natalie Piccotti, Director of Marketing
Kassie Graves, Vice President of Editorial
Jamie Giganti, Director of Academic Publishing

Cover image source: U. S. Department of State, "John Kennedy, Nikita Khrushchev 1961," https://commons.wikimedia.org/wiki/File:John_Kennedy%2C_Nikita_Khrushchev_1961. jpg, 1961.

Printed in the United States of America.

ISBN: 978-1-5165-2027-5 (pbk) / 978-1-5165-2028-2 (br)

The Cold War

A Battle of Global Ideologies

First Edition

Peter Tsahiridis

Missouri State University

To my wife, Kristine, my children, Dimitri, Madeleine, and Gwendolyn.

Table of Contents

Introduction

The Cold War, the Battle of Global Ideologies, is designed to accommodate the learner as a refresher of the Cold War. As time goes on, society has acquired new meanings and new ideas concerning the Cold War, mostly drawn from political and ideological considerations. *The Cold War* takes an objective look at the events that caused the increasing tensions between the primary players of the Cold War, namely the United States and the Union of Soviet Socialist Republics (USSR). Each chapter of *The Cold War* is split into sections, which contain a focus question, the historical text, discussion questions, and a comparative essay. The focus question orients the reader to the historic impact that the superpowers had on the world and is the underlying theme throughout the chapter. This is followed by the historical text over the period discussed, along with integrative detailed notes. Following the historical text is a series of discussion questions, which provokes further discussion over the time period. Lastly, there is a comparative essay section, which allows for the learner to relate the historic period discussed in order to connect with more recent events in history. Making relevant, historical connections between events develops the analytical processes within a learner, which will aid in formulating a proper, logical interpretation of the events.

Although there were other events that occurred to increase the tensions between the two world powers, the United States and the USSR, the historic events discussed in this book clearly illustrate that there was an interdependence connecting those events, which created accumulated affects that ultimately ended the Cold War. When did the Cold War officially start? The standoff between the United States and the Soviet Union started, oddly enough, with the dropping of the atomic bombs in August of 1945 from an

American B-29 bomber causing the annihilation of the Japanese cities of Hiroshima and Nagasaki. Such actions forced the Soviet Union to respond to the new American threat.[1]

The race over ideologies between the United States, a capitalistic society, and that of the USSR, a Communistic society, would be fought impetuously on the distant lands of other countries like Greece, Korea, Hungary, Cuba, Vietnam, and Afghanistan. Understanding the events of the Cold War can help us as individuals appreciate the new dynamics that we are facing in the 21st century. The breakup of countries into smaller ones, the regional civil strife over limited resources, the increasing plight of third world populations, the increase in refugee migrations, the return to longstanding historical conflicts, and the rearming of nuclear arsenals are all a result of the end of the Cold War. Through the lessons learned during the Cold War (1945-1991), has it transformed American, European, and Russian governments? Will the institutions of the Cold War remain during the latter part of the 21st century, or will a new global threat arise? The agglomeration of weapons from rogue third world nations will increase, but be sold and regulated by first world powers who are desperate to increase their economic status to compete for the limited resources available on Earth. The first world powers' goal of unobtainability of nuclear weapons by totalitarian and theocratic nations will direct the geopolitical policies and practices of the new economic world that has detached itself from the remnants of the Cold War to one that safeguards the trade secrets and multibillion-dollar contractional agreements between corporations and nations throughout the world. National security was the primary apparatus through which nations like the United States and the USSR implemented their ideological cause throughout rogue nations like Korea and Vietnam, yet in the 21st century, such causes are consequent to the rising capitalistic opportunities that can benefit a nation in the new world economic order. Throughout the history of the Cold War, a time arose that lent a sense of leadership to those men and women with the fortitude and tenacity to stand up for what was in the name of humanity all that was good and all that represented the drive and force to acquire and maintain a free world. By driving away the forces of subjugation and economic oppression, the call of freedom and the ideas of capitalism

---

1   According to Isaac Deutscher and his book entitled *Stalin*, from 1948 through the 1950s Stalin maintained a Red Army of 5.5 million troops to counter the American nuclear supremacy. The plan was to flood Germany and the West with a horde of troops to counter the Truman Doctrine; this was a plausible deterrent from the Americans' impending threat.

eventually reigned throughout the world. In the 21st century, the nations of the world have once again been plagued by the ideas of nationalism, economics, and human expansion; yet our sense of humanity has dwindled and our in-action in places like Syria during its civil war have only emboldened the expansion of primitive reasoning. Capitalism has been replaced by economic expediency, and Communism has been replaced by the evoking of a world that once was, but can never be.

Chapter 1

The Potsdam Declaration, the Ending of Wartime Alliances, and the Beginning of Cold War Rivalries

Chapter Focus

How do you think the United States impacted the rest of the world between 1945 and 1961? Can you give any specific examples? How do you think the USSR impacted the rest of the world during the same time period? Can you give any specific examples?

The surrender of Hitler's Germany in May of 1945 met the immediate attention of the Allied Powers. The Allied Powers consisted of President Harry S. Truman[1] of the United States, Chiang Kai-shek of China, the Soviet premier Joseph Stalin of the Union of Soviet Socialist Republics, and Prime Minister Winston Churchill of Great Britain, who responded in July 1945 at the capital city of Potsdam of the German Federal State of Brandenburg to proclaim to the Japanese government their unconditional surrender.[2] After the dropping of the atomic bombs on the Japanese cities of Hiroshima and Nagasaki, the Supreme Commander of the Allied Powers,

---

1   According to Tamara L. Roleff, book editor of *The Atomic Bomb*, the dropping of the atomic bomb under the orders of President Truman was so controversial that a transfer of power from the military to the civilian side of government took place when Congress created the Atomic Energy Commission (AEC) in 1946.

2   The United States one day before the Potsdam Conference tested the atomic bomb successfully in Alamogordo, New Mexico, and according to Brian Moynahan in his book entitled *Claws of the Bear: The History of the Red Army from the Revolution to the Present*, President Truman informed Stalin of their new weapon. Stalin seemed to be indifferent to it.

General Douglas MacArthur, accepted the surrender of the Japanese government by September of 1945.[3]

The dropping of the atomic bombs on Japan forced the Japanese government to surrender, as a result, instantly cutting the ties of power between the alliance of the United States and the Soviets. No longer would the United States need the USSR to help them eradicate the Japanese military. The dropping of the atomic bomb launched the United States into the atomic era. The aspirations of other nations sought the secret to the new weapon. Julius and Ethel Rosenberg and a band of conspirators who were associated with the secret development of the weapon were charged with espionage in 1951. Both Julius and Ethel were put to death two years later. Within that short time frame, from 1945 to 1953, the Soviet Union managed to conduct its own nuclear testing by 1949.

The United States was not the sole nuclear power and had to share the rest of the world with the Soviet Union. However, even before the trial of Julius and Ethel Rosenberg and before the dropping of the atomic bombs on the Japanese cities of Hiroshima and Nagasaki, in 1940, under the scientific leadership of Igor Kurchatov, the Soviet Union directed the Leningrad Physical-Technical Institute, the Radium Institute, and the Leningrad Institute of Physical Chemistry to research the methods of developing a uranium/plutonium type of bomb. The Russian scientists openly published the material on the separation of isotopes, the production of heavy water, and nuclear fission.[4] Not long after, N.N. Semenov, director of the Leningrad Institute

---

3   After the dropping of the atomic bombs, Dr. R.F. Bacher, chief scientist at Los Alamos and professor of physics at Cornell University, Dr. A. H. Compton, director of the University of Chicago Metallurgical Project where the development of plutonium occurred, Dr. E. O. Lawrence, director of the University of California Radiation Laboratory charged with magnetic methods of separating Uranium-235, Dr. J.R. Oppenheimer, director of the Los Alamos Laboratory where the atomic bomb was being developed and professor of physics at California Institute of Technology in Pasadena, California, Dr. F.H. Spedding, professor of chemistry and director of Iowa State College Laboratory where uranium metal was developed, Dr. H.C. Urey, nuclear physicist at the University of Chicago who developed a method of separating Uranium-235, and Dr. Richard C. Tolman, scientific adviser to Major General Grooves and vice-chairman of the National Defense Research Committee constructed a letter on February 4, 1946, to Major General L.R. Grooves to release the scientific and technical data concerning the atomic bomb in order to enhance US security. World War II was over; therefore, either the scientists wanted to accept the proper accolades for the development of the atomic bomb or, what was more reasonable to believe, was that the scientists felt remorse and even guilt for allowing the military to use the weapon and wanted Soviet scientists to even the balance of power through their own development of the atomic bomb (Declassification, 1946).

4   The development of the nuclear bomb by the Soviet Union was brilliantly analyzed by the author Brian Moynahan in his book entitled *Claws of the Bear: The History of the Red Army from*

of Physical Chemistry, won a Nobel Prize for his work in chemical reactions.[5] What we can really conclude from this section was that the idea of an atomic bomb was researched since the 1930s, and the ideas and research were shared among scientists until the US and British governments decided to make it secret because of the continuing war with Germany and Japan. Although Soviet scientists like N.N. Semenov were leaders in their field, they did not have the resources allotted to them like the United States when it came to weapons development. However, with such a lack of resources, the Soviet scientists adapted to their situation and proceeded in making a lethal atomic weapon to showcase to the United States of America in August of 1949.[6]

Postwar Years in Europe and Japan: The End of Days

Postwar Europe and Japan suffered from the allied atomic bombings and mass-carpet bombings that occurred in Dresden, Germany, and in Tokyo, Japan. These types of aerial bombings had a singular purpose: a psychological destruction of the enemy. The question to ask is whether these types of attacks were responsible on behalf of America and its allies. Whatever the reasons and justifications for mass killings at the end of World War II, the

---

the *Revolution to the Present*, where he stressed how Joseph Stalin, leader of the Soviet Union, was furious that the United States and the British were secretly developing an atomic weapon. However, the Soviet Union had to worry about the advancing German forces under Adolph Hitler in his most ambitious military venture called Operation Barbarossa.

5   According to NobelPrize.org, Sir Cyril Norman Hinshelwood and N.N. Semenov won the Nobel Prize in 1956 because of their work on the mechanisms of chemical reactions. N.N. Semenov discussed his research in a paper entitled *Some Problems Relating to Chain Reactions and to the Theory of Combustion* located on (Semenov, 1946). Although he served as director of the Leningrad Institute of Physical Chemistry, he spent most of his time in his laboratory at Leningrad Physical-Technical Institute and the Institute of Chemical Physics in the Academy of Sciences where he focused on the phenomena of the combustion process; utilizing the concept, he established Arrhenius's law, which summarizes that heat that is generated from a chemical reaction itself increases the velocity of the reaction.

6   This information was discussed further in a January 4, 1993, *New York Times* article by Serge Schmemann entitled "Soviet A-Bomb Built from U.S. Data, Russian Says." In this article Schmemann reports that Soviet spies stole secrets about the atomic bomb from the Americans and that is how the Soviets were able to catch up in the atomic age. However, this does not seem plausible since the Soviets had been researching aspects of nuclear fission since the 1930s and published their material on the subject. The more plausible explanation is that the United States was under a time crunch to end the war with Japan and with the cooperation of the British stole industrial and scientific secrets of the Soviets.

Soviet Union was encouraged to stop the Allied advance. This became more evident as both the Allies and the Soviet Union rushed to take control of Berlin, Germany. Germany was a tantrum of trouble for both the West and the East. Within the 20th century, Germany viscerally organized its military, caused two world wars, and wreaked havoc upon Europe and Russia. The Soviets, under Joseph Stalin, wanted a protective barrier between the Soviet Union and Germany. With the mass flooding of Russian troops into Europe, their destination was Berlin, Germany.[7]

Berlin, the epicenter of destruction, where the Allies controlled the western part of Europe and Berlin and the Soviets controlled the eastern part of Europe and Berlin. The psychological impact of massive destruction, the images of gruesome deaths, and the lack of modern resources obligated European civilians to choose between the ideology of the West (mainly unrestricted freedom and capitalism) or that of the East (extreme socialism run by totalitarianism). No matter what ideology that European civilians desired, the need to be fed and protected was paramount as uprisings and leftist guerrilla factions were forming against existing conservative governments, more notably in Greece from 1945 to 1947. The situation in Europe was worsening with the increased influence of the Soviet Union; the United States needed to act. Harry S. Truman, who served as president of the United States from 1945 to 1953, declared in his 1947 speech to Congress an ideological war against the Soviet Union, where he addressed the situation in Greece and Turkey:

> [...] if Turkey is to have the assistance it needs, the United States must supply it. We are the only country able to provide that help [...] if we falter in our leadership, we may endanger the peace in our world—and we shall surely endanger the welfare of this nation. Great responsibilities have been placed upon us by the swift movement of events. I am confident that the Congress will face these responsibilities squarely.[8]

---

7   The Soviets under Stalin could give the Allies of the West all sorts of trouble, and from June 24, 1948, to May 12, 1949, the Soviet Union blockaded all resources into Allied-controlled West Berlin. However, the actions taken by the Soviet Union only proved that the Western powers through their airlift capabilities could sustain a long-term operation and continue feeding and supplying the West Berliners. Allied planes were landing every 45 seconds at Tempelhof Airport (US Department of State).

8   This speech is located at the Harry S. Truman Library and Museum archive website at (Truman, 1947).

The new international responsibility of the United States was now focused on fighting the development of Communism and assisting in the humanitarian crisis in Europe. The fighting of Communism was essential to President Truman and was eventually dubbed the Truman Doctrine. Under order by President Harry S. Truman, Congress approved the Economic Corporation Act of 1948, dubbed the Marshall Plan.[9] Under the direction of Secretary of State George C. Marshall, the war-torn countries of Europe including Great Britain received over $12 billion in US foreign aid. Meanwhile, the United States and its allies of the Western nations formed NATO (North Atlantic Treaty Organization). This was an attempt to formalize political and ideological beliefs against the Soviet Union, which eventually responded in 1955 with the Warsaw Pact.[10]

The Korean War, a New Type of Battle

After the Japanese surrendered in 1945, Russia launched an attack against Japan's previously held territories of Manchuria and Korea. In the case of

---

9   The Marshall Plan, created by Secretary of State George C. Marshall, formulated a plan to recover the parts of Germany and Europe under Allied control. According to Brian Moynahan, in his book entitled *Claws of the Bear: The History of the Red Army from the Revolution to the Present*, he had figured that the United States spent over $13 billion in monies to the western nations of Europe. This cost has been confirmed by the President Truman Museum and Library (Harry S. Truman Library and Museum). Secretary of State George Marshall gave a speech at Harvard University on the Marshall Plan. At Harvard's commencement speech in June of 1947, Secretary of State George Marshall addressed the Harvard Alumni Association, where he laid out his Marshall Plan to rejuvenate the economies of Western Europe (Marshall, 1947). In Marshall's Harvard speech, he recognized the reasonableness and intelligence of his audience, but also puts blame on the media for not explaining the situation in Europe in a comprehensible way that the average American citizen could understand. Marshall also feels because of the geographic distance of the United States that her citizens could never really feel the desperation of the western Europeans. This speech was important because Marshall discussed how Nazi rule, before and during the war, put such a stranglehold on the macro and micro economies of Europe that these distressed societies were literally in shambles. Marshall clearly advocated for American aid to Europe for the sole purpose of establishing their economies so that those Western nations in Europe can begin the process of renewal with their own citizens. Marshall did not want to stay in Europe for the long haul; he believed that the Europeans should guide their own reconstruction. Oddly, Marshall never mentions the Soviet Union in his speech. This may be an indication that Marshall may not have agreed with the Truman Doctrine, which advocated taking on the Soviet Union whenever and wherever possible.

10   In the North Atlantic Treaty established in Washington, DC, on April 4, 1949, article five states, "The Parties agree that an armed attack against one or more of them in Europe or North America shall be considered an attack against them all and consequently they agree that, if such an armed attack occurs, each of them, in exercise of the right of individual or collective

Korea, the Soviet armies held the northern part while the United States held the southern part of Korea, divided by the 38th parallel. The newly created United Nations recognized the ROK (Republic of Korea) headed by the nationalist leader Syngman Rhee, and set up Seoul as its capital. In response, by 1948 the DPRK (Democratic People's Republic of Korea) headed by Kim Il-Sung of the central government adopted the Communist platform and made Pyongyang its capital. In June of 1950, the DPRK (North Korea) invaded the ROK (South Korea).[11] In the US Resolutions 82 & 83 of June 1950, Present Harry S. Truman stated in part,

> *Determines this action constitutes a breach of peace; and calls for the immediate cessation of hostilities; calls upon the authorities of North Korea to withdraw forthwith their armed forces to the 38th parallel ... Recommends that the Members of the United Nations furnish such assistance to the Republic of Korea as may be necessary to repel the armed attack and to restore international peace and security in the area.*[12]

The United States was obligated by the United Nations Security Council in a unanimous vote to come to the aid of South Korea. President Harry S. Truman, upholding his own doctrine, responded by sending American forces to the region. Although the fighting lasted from 1950 to 1953, ending in a stalemate between the divided nation, President Truman's actions to send troops to Korea was probably in response from his lack of support to the Chinese nationalists headed by

---

self-defense recognized by Article 51 of the Charter of the United Nations, will assist the Party or Parties so attacked by taking forthwith, individually and in concert with the other Parties, such action as it deems necessary, including the use of armed force, to restore and maintain the security of the North Atlantic area (NATO, 1949)."

11   According to Isaac Deutscher and his book entitled *Stalin*, the Soviet member of the Council walked out of a Security Council meeting concerning US involvement in Korea. Instead, Stalin ordered arms and munitions to help support the North Koreans and the Chinese volunteers, but did not commit Soviet troops to the area. Stalin was more concerned with the Soviet economy and decided to invest in the nuclear industry whereby 1953 the Soviets manufactured their first hydrogen bomb. The directive to increase the Soviet nuclear capabilities undermined the efforts of the Soviet consumer economy where Soviet citizens acquired only one-quarter to one-third of the consumer products of American citizens; and with increased urbanization and shortage of housing, the Soviet government could do little to nothing to help its citizen population.

12   (NATO, 1949)

Chiang Kai-shek, who lost to the Communist revolutionary leader Mao Zedong in the Chinese revolution of 1949. Despite the motivations of President Truman, the Korean War lent itself to unforgettable military campaigns between the Allies, the United States, and the Republic of Korea (ROK) against North Korea.[13] Hundreds of thousands of North Korean People's Army (NKPA) crossed the 38th parallel and captured the capital city of Seoul and pushed the Allies back, where they steadfastly held back the advances of the NKPA at the Pusan Perimeter from August to September of 1950.[14]

Pusan was a major seaport for Korea, located at the southeastern tip of the peninsula; however, that pentacle was too ambitious even for North Korea as the US and ROK forces eventually pushed the North Korean army back to their capital of Pyongyang. The Korean War was for the first time a test of American restraint, unlike previously in World War II where the principle of mass was used to commit naval, air, and ground troops unrestrictedly upon the enemy. Ruminants of World War II like that of General Douglas MacArthur, US commander of the Army, had a difficult time adjusting to the United Nations–driven Korean War with its international laws and rules of engagement. Although General MacArthur was successful in commanding US forces combined with ROK forces on the landing of Inch'on pushing onto North Korean territory and by the end of September recaptured the South Korean capital of Seoul. It was evident that President Truman wanted to follow the international rules of engagement and conflicted with General MacArthur's cavalier World War II style. In April of 1951 President Truman relieved General MacArthur because of MacArthur's ambitions to commit to a full-scale war with China.[15] The Korean War is significant because it illustrated that the American military

---

13   The Korean War issue set up the platform for then congressman Richard Nixon's senatorial campaign against Congresswoman Helen Gahagan Douglas, who opposed the existence of a Communist threat to America. Even John F. Kennedy donated $1,000 to Congressman Nixon's senatorial campaign against Helen Douglas (Richard Nixon Foundation, 2017).

14   According to W.W. Rostow in his book entitled *The Dynamics of Soviet Society*, the Soviet Union ostentatiously presented to the world its propaganda of peace, welfare, and civil liberty while surreptitiously committing to two goals: (1) splitting the relations of the United States from her European Allies and (2) continuing a policy of expansion without being involved in a major conflict.

15   Truman relieved General MacArthur, a very popular wartime general who understood the greater military strategy against Communism, China. According to Bob Considine in his book entitled *General Douglas MacArthur*, General MacArthur knew China was the greatest threat to the US position in Asia and wanted an economic blockade of all China ports, increased

could be curtailed by its civilian government. Furthermore, the United States was willing to join with the international community concerning issues that arose in Asia. During the Korean conflict, the United Nations Security Council was becoming the premier legal and moral standard for the world to emulate. No longer would a US president during the Cold War period ever go to the US Congress for a declaration of war against an enemy.[16]

Red Scare in America

Other pressures such as the HUAC (House Un-American Activities Committee) developed in 1938[17] and their investigations to find Communists in America by targeting the influential people of the motion picture industry by 1947 led to convictions on contempt of Congress charges for the unwillingness to answer questions. As a result, the congressional investigations caused a Hollywood blacklist to arise. These actors, directors, screenwriters, and artists were blacklisted from the Hollywood industry in fear of further prosecution from Congress and negative ratings from the public. Actors and

---

reconnaissance of specific areas in China to include Manchuria, and an end of the appeasement policy with China.

16   Article 1, Section 8 of the US Constitution states that it has the power to declare war, grant letters of marque and reprisal, and make rules concerning captures on land and water.

17   HUAC had such influence on the American political system that even President Roosevelt believed in the threat to communism; he signed into law the Smith Act, also known as the Alien Registration Act of 1940, which served as a legal device to prosecute members of the Communist Party. However, this law was limited under the US Supreme Court ruling of *Yates v. United States*, 1957 (Alien Registration Act of 1940). The limitations in part stated in section 1: "Since the Communist Party came into being in 1945, and the indictment was not returned until 1951, the three-year statute of limitations had run on the 'organizing' charge, and required the withdrawal of that part of the indictment from the jury's consideration. Pp. 303–312. [354 U.S. 298, 299]; (a) Applying the rule that criminal statutes are to be construed strictly, the word 'organize, as used in the Smith Act, is construed as referring only to acts entering into the creation of a new organization, and not to acts thereafter performed in carrying on its activities, even though the latter may loosely be termed 'organizational.'" Pp. 303–311; and section 2: "The Smith Act does not prohibit advocacy and teaching of forcible overthrow of the Government as an abstract principle, divorced from any effort to instigate action to that end; the trial court's charge to the jury furnished wholly inadequate guidance on this central point in the case; and the conviction cannot be allowed to stand. Dennis v. United States, 341 U.S. 494, distinguished. Pp. 312–327." (Yates v. United States, 1957).

political activists offered testimony before the committee. Ronald Reagan, in answering Chief Investigator Mr. Stripling:

> Mr. STRIPLING: "Mr. Reagan, what is your feeling about what steps should be taken to rid the motion-picture industry of any Communist influences, if they are there?"
>
> Mr. REAGAN: "Well, sir ... 99 percent of us are pretty well aware of what is going on, and I think within the bounds of our democratic rights, and never once stepping over the rights given us by democracy, we have done a pretty good job in our business of keeping those people's activities curtailed. After all, we must recognize them at present as a political party. On that basis, we have exposed their lies when we came across them, we have opposed their propaganda, and I can certainly testify that in the case of the Screen Actors Guild we have been eminently successful in preventing them from, with their usual tactics, trying to run a majority of an organization with a well-organized minority.
>
> So, that fundamentally I would say in opposing those people that the best thing to do is to make democracy work. In the Screen Actors Guild, we make it work by insuring everyone a vote and by keeping everyone informed. I believe that, as Thomas Jefferson put it, if all the American people know all of the facts they will never make a mistake.
>
> Whether the party should be outlawed, I agree with the gentlemen that preceded me that that is a matter for the Government to decide. As a citizen, I would hesitate, or not like, to see any political party outlawed on the basis of its political ideology. We have spent 170 years in this country on the basis that democracy is strong enough to stand up and fight against the inroads of any ideology. However, if it is proven that an organization is an agent of a power, a foreign power, or in any way not a legitimate political party, and I think the Government is capable of proving that, if the proof is there, then that is another matter ...
>
> I happen to be very proud of the industry in which I work; I happen to be very proud of the way in which we conducted the fight. I do not believe the Communists have ever at any time

Ronald Reagan, "House Committee on Un-American Activities (HUAC) Testimony," 1947.

been able to use the motion picture screen as a sounding board for their philosophy or ideology ..."[18]

With Hollywood working against each other, most writers had to surreptitiously write under false names and work through a Hollywood black market system. The most prominent of these blacklisted Hollywood Ten, as they were called, was the Oscar-winning screenwriter and Academy Award winner Dalton Trumbo for his work on *Roman Holiday* (1953) and *The Brave One* (1956). Through those years of working in the Hollywood black market system, the success of HUAC was confirmed by the espionage trial of Alger Hiss, a member of the State Department, who was substantiated by Whittaker Chambers, a defecting Soviet spy, who helped condemn Alger Hiss and his Communist plot against the United State. A young congressman by the name of Richard M. Nixon led the investigation against Alger Hiss. By 1948, Congressman Nixon, member of the HUAC, used the power of television to reveal the espionage committed by Alger Hiss. Nixon stated for a television audience,

> *I am holding in my hand a microfilm of very highly confidential secret state department documents. These documents were fed out of the state department over ten years ago, by Communists who were employees of that department and who were interested in seeing these documents were sent to the Soviet Union, where the interests of the Soviet Union happen to be in conflict with those of the United States.*[19]

The testimony of Whittaker Chambers and his rendition of the "concealed enemy" in which all of the United States was fighting indicated that Alger Hiss[20] was committing perjury before the congressional committee. Hiss

---

18   Reagan Foundation.

19   By the Associated Press archive (Universal Newsreels Outtakes, 2016).

20   The entire Hiss debacle was an embarrassment for President Harry S. Truman; as a result, in 1949 Truman authorized the Justice Department under the Smith Act to go after Communists; this led to the 1950s case in the US Supreme Court, *Dennis v. United States*. Stated in part: "Petitioners, leaders of the Communist Party in this country, were indicted in a federal district court under § 3 of the Smith Act for willfully and knowingly conspiring (1) to organize as the Communist Party a group of persons to teach and advocate the overthrow and destruction of the Government of the United States by force and violence, and (2) knowingly and willfully to advocate and teach the duty and necessity of overthrowing and destroying the Government of the United States by force and violence. The trial judge instructed the jury that they could not

was sent to prison for perjury, not espionage; however, this episode in the United States paved the way for more Communist investigations under Senator Joseph McCarthy. Republican Senator Joseph McCarthy from 1950 to 1954 went before the public to announce that the State Department was harboring Communists and that the US Army was soft on Communism. This was somewhat of a political liability for the new Republican president.

The Eisenhower Policy of Containment

Dwight D. Eisenhower carried on the Truman doctrine of directly confronting Communism to one of containment. The Eisenhower presidency ran from 1953 to 1961, and unlike Eisenhower's predecessor, Harry Truman, Eisenhower kept America in relative peace with the Soviet Union. Eisenhower's New Look policy moved away from the tactical conventions of military buildup and the pleasing of the military industrial complex to one of dependence on a nuclear buildup. However, this haphazardly increased the tensions on both sides by undergoing a massive buildup of nuclear weapons, a strategy known as mutually assured destruction, or MAD.

In his January 20, 1953, inaugural address, President Eisenhower states in part:

> My fellow citizens [...] forces of good and evil are [...] armed and opposed [...] We are called as a people to give testimony in the sight of the world to our faith that the future shall belong to the free [...] The enemies of this faith, know no God [...] we face the threat [...] with confidence and conviction.[21]

The newly elected president was addressing the fight against Communism. President Eisenhower vilified the Communists and put the burden of responsibility on the American people to fight the injustice of anyone or any idea that hampers freedom around the world. Eisenhower's containment policies assured the Soviet Union that the United States was ready to strike

---

convict unless they found that petitioners intended to overthrow the Government 'as speedily as circumstances would permit,' but that, if they so found, then, as a matter of law, there was sufficient danger of a substantive evil that Congress has a right to prevent to justify application of the statute under the First Amendment. Petitioners were convicted. (Dennis v. U.S., 1951)."

21   C-Span Archives.

back with nuclear force many times over. With the death of Joseph Stalin in 1953, the new Soviet leader, Nikita Khrushchev, opened up to the United States diplomatically, a policy known as *détente*. However, détente offered little when it came to smaller conflicts that arose; for example, in 1956 a revolt in Hungary broke out, and the USSR sent in military units to quash it, causing death and destruction. President Eisenhower's administration refrained from taking any direct military action.

Rather, President Eisenhower took this burden of responsibility by using clandestine tactics to engage the spread of Communism. Eisenhower employed the Central Intelligence Agency to undermine established governments in Central and South America, Cuba, Egypt, Congo, Lebanon,[22] and Iran. The secret military support and monies to governments that supported American ideologies of freedom and democracy were really a cover-up to protect American oil interests overseas.

In May 1960, an American U-2 plane was shot down by Russian air defense.[23] Not only did first secretary of the USSR Nikita Khrushchev capture the downed spy plane, he produced the American pilot, Major Francis Gary Powers, forcing President Eisenhower to admit to the world that America intentionally spied on Russia. Francis Gary Powers was placed on trial in Russia, and five months later Khrushchev went to the UN to further criticize the United States with his infamous statement, "I will bury you." Whatever the meaning of his statement, it was clear to Khrushchev that Communism would outlast capitalism and further illustrate that the United States would not relent to Communistic pressures. President Eisenhower, however, followed his policy of containment to match Communism wherever it spread in the world and employed the CIA to undercut anticapitalistic governments around the world. However, a new era in space was about to

---

22   President Eisenhower sent US Marines to Lebanon in 1958, partly to test the Eisenhower Doctrine, which stated in part, "To secure and protect the territorial integrity and political independence of such nations, requesting such aid against overt armed aggression from any nation controlled by international Communism," and because the president of Lebanon requested military aid to stop his Communist political rivals (US Department of State).

23   President Eisenhower commissioned the company Lockheed to develop the U-2, a reconnaissance aircraft capable of reaching over 80,000 feet. Unbeknownst to the United States, the Soviets were able to track U-2 flights that started in 1956. Then on May 1, 1960, the USSR shot down Major Powers' U-2 as he was over the Soviet Union on the eve of a European summit in Paris where President Eisenhower, France's president de Gaulle, Britain's prime minister Macmillan, and Khrushchev were supposed to meet (NASA). Oddly, according to *The Warren Report*, the Department of State revealed that Lee Harvey Oswald's defection to the Soviet Union was in 1959 and his return to the United States was in 1962.

begin as the Soviet Union illustrated its superiority by launching *Sputnik*, its first satellite into space, in 1957. In addition, the National Aeronautics and Space Administration (NASA), which was launched in 1958, was already thinking ahead in space technologies by trying to convince President Eisenhower that cooperative programs with the Soviets was possible, especially with meteorological satellites; this project was dubbed Project Comet.[24]

Chapter 1: Identify the Following Key Players and Events

- The Potsdam Declaration
  - Igor Kurchatov
- Joseph Stalin
  - The Greek Uprising of 1945–1947
- Alger Hiss
  - U-2 Spy Plane
- Khrushchev
  - Major Francis Gary Powers
- Truman Doctrine
  - New Look Policy
- HUAC
  - Mao Zedong

Discussion Questions

With the focus questions in mind, try to see the discussion questions from a neutral and objective point of view. This may be difficult at first, but it also may give new insight into the situation that was occurring during this time and more importantly will add a sense of reasonableness to your logical way of thinking.

1. What happened with US and USSR relations after the Potsdam Declaration?
2. Why was the Korean War different from World War II?

---

24 Even the car company Chrysler was trying to get into the space race and was particularly interested in the development of the *Saturn S-IV*. The space race was big business, and bids were on the table ranging from $24 million to $138 million. Companies, organizations, and academics like the RAND Corporation, the Brookings Institution, and MIT all wanted to be part of the social and economic opportunities that a new frontier could bring. In May of 1960, Congress was projected to give NASA some $915 million (NASA).

3. Was the paranoia that surrounded what was known as the "Red Scare" justified?
4. Why did Soviet premier Nikita Khrushchev invoke a hardline stance against the United States under President Eisenhower?
5. What comparison could you make about President Truman's administration and President Eisenhower's administration?

Comparative Essay

Directions: Read the following passage and write an essay that compares the actions of the United States during the Cold War to those that occurred after the attack on 9/11 against the World Trade Center. Are there any similarities in the US government's behavior?

In 1947, President Harry S. Truman signed the Federal Employee Loyalty Program under Executive Order 9835 to purge suspected individuals of being disloyal to the government. This was furthered in 1950 by the US Congress as they passed a security program statute that stated any government employee could be dismissed in the interest of national security; this was continued by executive order from President Eisenhower.[25] The creation of HUAC (House Un-American Activities Committee) and later the granting of relentless power to Senator McCarthy in his anti-Communist crusade, coupled with Congress passing the Communist Control Act,[26] indicated that the reality in the United States was fear of Communism. The anxiety of a Communist takeover prompted Presidents Truman and Eisenhower to engage in direct and indirect actions around the world in combating Communist maneuvers. The impact that both the United States and the USSR made from 1945–1961 divided the world into that which was free and embraced capitalism to that which was not free and embraced Communism. Missed opportunities for both superpowers to embrace China caused more division, as China was fighting for its own Communist identity and expansion, only to be blocked both by the USSR and the United States. Once the

---

25 S. Sheldon Weinhaus in an article entitled *The Federal Employee Loyalty-Security Program: A Critique*; in his article, it seemed that no government entity was willing to dismiss the premise of Communist infiltration in the US government. http://openscholarship.wustl.edu/cgi/viewcontent.cgi?article=3425&context=law_lawreview

26 The Communist Control Act of 1954 ensured that the rights of US citizens could be stripped if they were ever involved with the overthrow of the government. https://www.law.cornell.edu/uscode/text/50/842

superpowers established that neither side could push the other out, most notably in Korea, this allowed for other opportunities to spread their ideologies in places like Cuba and Vietnam.

Time Line

- 1938—House Un-American Activities Committee (HUAC) is created
- 1945—Germany surrenders
- 1945—Potsdam Conference
- 1945—General Douglas MacArthur accepts surrender of Japanese government
- 1947—President Harry S. Truman pledges to help Greece and Turkey fight against Communism
- 1948—Soviet blockade of West Berlin
- 1948—Congressman Nixon, member of HUAC, reveals evidence of Alger Hiss
- 1949—Soviets conduct nuclear testing
- 1949—NATO is established
- 1950—North Korean People's Army (NKPA) crosses 38th parallel
- 1950—Senator Joseph McCarthy accuses the US State Department of harboring Communists
- 1951—Julius and Ethel Rosenberg charged with espionage
- 1953—Eisenhower gives presidential inaugural address about fighting Communism
- 1953—Soviets manufacture first hydrogen bomb
- 1955—Warsaw Pact is created
- 1956—Soviets invade the country of Hungary and quell revolt
- 1960—Russian air defense systems shoot down U-2 spy plane

Chapter 2

The Kennedy Administration, 1961–1963

A Crisis Abroad

Chapter Focus

Did the Kennedy administration take the proper steps when dealing with the Cuban Missile Crisis? Can you give any specific examples? How do you think the USSR was perceived after the Cuban Missile Crisis? Can you give any specific examples?

U nder joint military jurisdiction, Berlin was split between the Allies (France, Britain, and the United States) and the Soviet Union. The Soviet Russian government under Joseph Stalin sacrificed greatly to take over Berlin, the stronghold of its nemesis, Adolf Hitler. From 1949 to 1960, Germans in the millions from East Berlin fled into West Berlin. The flooding of Germans from East to West put at risk the Communist regime economically in East Germany. Without a steady labor force, the East Germans would collapse. The Soviet Union under Khrushchev directed the East German government to begin construction of a barrier/wall. Khrushchev used this opportunity to test the newly elected US president John F. Kennedy. By April of 1961, the Soviet Union launched their first man into space, cosmonaut Yuri Gagarin. As President Eisenhower had to answer the Soviet challenge to space, so would the newly elected US president, John F. Kennedy. Furthermore, in August of 1961, the East Germans with the help of Soviet Russia began building the Berlin Wall. President Kennedy failed to act when he had the opportunity to crush the wall through military action.

Instead, the Kennedy administration decided to make it a political apex in the world of politics.

The presidential inaugural address of John F. Kennedy rushed in a new era of postwar energy and optimism. Kennedy, a veteran of World War II, was an exceptionally bright individual who thought of the world as interconnected; he refused to be subjugated to the anachronistic thinking of his predecessors. Kennedy was aware that his words and actions represented US policy and that the enemies of the United States would respect or at least acknowledge possible US reprisal. Kennedy's inability to act while the Berlin Wall was being created was measured by the possible response to the USSR; that which would eventually lead to nuclear war. Both superpowers had the capability to launch nuclear weapons and end all life as we know it on Earth. American as well as Soviet citizens were in a state of anxiety; however, the tensions created by both Soviet and American actions tested the resolve of both nations. To further compound the nuclear threat, the Soviets launched cosmonaut Yuri Gagarin in April of 1961. A month later, the Kennedy administration ordered astronaut Alan Shepard into space, where he completed a 15-minute orbital flight; by February 1962, astronaut John Glenn had successfully completed three orbits around the Earth in his spacecraft, *Friendship 7*.[1] The success of the Kennedy administration's policies during the space race were clear to the Soviet Union: that America would not stop its research and development (R&D) as was verified by Khrushchev's message to President Kennedy in February of 1962,

> In the nuclear rocket weapons age ... and we have entered this age ... the numerical strength of the forces does not by a long way have the importance it had in World Wars I and II. ... nuclear rocket weapons, with which the decisive blow can be struck even before vast armies can be mobilized and thrown into battle.[2]

These are even more clues as to why Khrushchev would try to arm Cuba with missiles that could strike the United States, and this was the essence of the Cuban Missile Crisis October 22, 1962.[3] The Soviet Union went from

---

1   John F. Kennedy Presidential Library and Museum, 2017.

2   Central Intelligence Agency, 1963.

3   In a secret CIA report over *Khrushchev's Role in the Current Controversy Over Soviet Defense Policy*, the Soviet strategic thinking in the wake of the aftermath of the Cuban Missile Crisis

a stance of "must always have superiority in armed forces" to one of parity with the West. This was done to salvage the hurt Soviet prestige during the Cuban Missile Crisis. Khrushchev believed in increasing the GNP of the Soviet Union; in fact, from 1955 to 1958, he reduced military expenditures by 2 billion rubles, and thus the GNP increased by 7 percent. This was primarily done because the investment in advanced weaponry (modernization) was very expensive. By 1958 the cost of research and development (R&D) and space costs dropped the GNP to around 4 or 5 percent. Khrushchev was willing to live with strategic inferiority, and putting weapons in Cuba was an inexpensive way to meet these demands to fulfill the strategic attack capability of the Soviet Union.

The dilemma was meeting military and economic requirements and pushing forward with the Soviet foreign policy. Khrushchev was now concerned about maintaining a large conventional force because it was hindering the economic security of the Soviet Union. Therefore, Khrushchev initially wanted to store weapons in Cuba to replace conventional troops and to keep the prowess on the imperial West. By January of 1960, Khrushchev initiated a depreciation of conventional troops. Khrushchev became an expert in shifting the monies from defense needs to consumer needs and vice versa. This was primarily done because the investment in advanced weaponry (modernization) was very expensive.

While Khrushchev was busy trying to balance the Soviet economy, the Bay of Pigs invasion into Cuba was beginning. The Bay of Pigs invasion of April 17, 1961, led by 1,400 anti-Castro Cuban exiles, landed on the southern coast of Cuba known as the Bay of Pigs.[4] This was an order signed by President Kennedy, but a program initiated by President Eisenhower. However, the leader of the Cuban people, the revolutionary Fidel Castro, was ready for the invasion, and because of physical mishaps and logistics, the landing

---

pointed out Khrushchev's objectives to secure a Soviet defense economic policy and keep up the present pace of Soviet armed strength. Khrushchev was now concerned about maintaining a large conventional force because it was hindering the economic security of the Soviet Union. Therefore, Khrushchev initially wanted to store weapons in Cuba to replace conventional troops and to keep the prowess on the imperial West. By January of 1960, Khrushchev initiated a depreciation of conventional troops. Khrushchev became an expert in shifting the monies from defense needs to consumer needs and vice versa. The Cuban Missile Crisis also portrayed the Soviet Union as adventurists willing to risk capitulation toward the West; at least that is what the Chinese thought.

4   https://www.jfklibrary.org/JFK/JFK-in-History/The-Bay-of-Pigs.aspx

was a failure, resulting in the capture and killing of the Cuban exiles.[5] It was Robert Kennedy who had to negotiate a settlement with Fidel Castro, an obvious sign of embarrassment for the United States.[6]

It is important to reiterate why the Cuban Missile Crisis even took place.[7] On February 27, 1962, Khrushchev again addressed the need to balance the economy and defense so that one factor of Soviet life did not overwhelm the other. Being overcommitted to defense showed in the Soviet economy, when by 1962, meat prices rose 30 percent, private housing construction slowed, and income tax incentives remained at a standstill.[8] The Cuban Missile Crisis occurred on October 22, 1962,[9] and was a fundamental challenge for the Soviet Union. Khrushchev, the leader of the Soviet Union, had to determine the best military strategy for the USSR as well as balance the economics of Soviet society. The most feasible strategy was to offset the contemporary Soviet military with nuclear weapons put in key positions around the world to better help the strategic advantage against the United States. The most feasible place was the island of Cuba. From April 14 to October 14, 1962, a military effort by the Soviets to put in place a nuclear offensive first-strike capability was being conducted in Cuba.

By March of 1962, the Central Intelligence Agency (CIA) increased its monthly overflights of Cuba to two flights per month.[10] The steps directed by the US intelligence agencies were to: (1) increase the number of agents inside of Cuba by making more use of legal travelers to Cuba; (2) use intelligence and security services from other countries; (3) increase the use of audio surveillance of any Cuban installations abroad; (4) increase the number of nonresident agents outside of Cuba to report on Cuban activities; (5) recruit personnel in commercial shipping to report on Cuban naval

---

5   http://nsarchive.gwu.edu/bayofpigs/19630400b.pdf

6   The CIA internal investigations of the Bay of Pigs invasion by the CIA historian Jack B. Pfeiffer noted that President Kennedy and General Maxwell Taylor ordered investigations about the failed attempt. General Taylor formed a Cuban Study Group (CSG) in which Attorney General Robert Kennedy was informed. R.F. Kennedy's group was known unpleasantly as the proctological group. https://www.cia.gov/library/readingroom/docs/C01254908.pdf

7   https://www.archives.gov/files/declassification/iscap/pdf/2011-063-doc4.pdf

8   Central Intelligence Agency, 1963.

9   In a secret CIA report over *Khrushchev's Role in the Current Controversy Over Soviet Defense Policy*, the Soviet strategic thinking in wake of the aftermath of the Cuban Missile Crisis pointed out Khrushchev's objectives to secure a Soviet defense economic policy and keep up the present pace of Soviet armed strength (Central Intelligence Agency, 1963).

10   Central Intelligence Agency, 1963.

activities; and (6) affiliate with illegal teams within Cuba to develop resistance and establish organized intelligence networks.[11] The intelligence mosaic, the collection of data from Cuba to the United States, consisted of human observation, modern technical devices, clandestine agents in Cuba, agents on commercial ships, refugees from Cuba, military officers in Cuba, travelers to and from Cuba, photographs taken from commercial ships, Cuban diplomats abroad, the intercept of communications, electronic emissions (SIGINT), press corps, radio and television, and overhead and peripheral reconnaissance.[12] Shipping intelligence marks the beginning of missile development.

Parts always need to be shipped: they are too large to transport by air; therefore, having a robust shipping intelligence can alert intelligence agencies of activities as they did during the Cuban Missile Crisis and the shipping of medium-range ballistic missiles (MRBMs).[13] Furthermore, any areas that are considered denied or restricted are areas of interest to intelligence agencies. At this time, there were many restricted areas in Cuba. In order to transmit messages on the activities within Cuba, agents used the open-mail system, wrote in secret languages, used radio transmissions, and arranged meetings with clandestine couriers. The United States would set up a base of operations for refugees; the state of Florida was the likely candidate for such a base of operations. Refugees from Cuba would be shuttled to the Caribbean Admission Center (CAC) at Opa-Locka Naval Air Station where they would be interviewed for any credible intelligence on the activities in Cuba.[14] Reports from refugees that the Soviets were

---

11   It was obvious that President Kennedy wanted to fix the Cuban problem and he wanted Castro out. Intelligence gathering and infiltration was done prior to any signs of Soviet military buildup (Central Intelligence Agency, 1963).

12   Personal note from Peter Tsahiridis: As I conducted research on this top-secret document, which was declassified on December 19, 2013, I started to reflect on my own intelligence background. The intelligence mosaic has become increasingly important to me personally and professionally. It describes how professionals should gather information for the use of making policy decisions. You need active participants and non-acting participants to support the claims associated with the objective. Never try to fit the objective to the facts; if you do it this way, you will always find the answer. This is a common mistake in intelligence; for example, "Will North Korea attack South Korea?" I can find almost any facts and/or intelligence that will support that decision. Let the facts speak for themselves, gather the information, support the information, verify the information, and then create a picture of activities that are occurring (Central Intelligence Agency, 1963).

13   MRBMs are usually set up around SAM sites, surface-to-air missiles.

14   Central Intelligence Agency, 1963.

providing sophisticated military equipment to the Cubans were verified in late August by U-2 reconnaissance missions. The US intelligence agencies also employed foreign diplomats with or without their knowing when gathering information about Cuba. Photographic and SIGINT materials were allocated from clandestine maritime operations to track Soviet ships going to Cuba.[15] Periphery intelligence is also important and occurred as much as possible during this time to monitor Cuban activities.[16]

Open-source intelligence increased at this time as well, which consisted of the participation of the Foreign Broadcast Information Division (FBID) and the Foreign Documents Division (FDD).[17] From the end of May to the beginning of October, the National Photographic Interpretation Center (NPIC) tried to verify more missile activity in Cuba, but to no avail.[18] The first piece of hard evidence arose on August 29, 1962, when a U-2 mission over Cuba confirmed eight SA-2 sites.[19] This news was reported from agents inside of Cuba by secret writing.[20] Other writings from agents in Havana

---

15 The hull of a ship must contain 70-foot hatches in order to hold MRBMs and IRBMs (intermediate-range ballistic missiles) (Central Intelligence Agency, 1963).

16 As part of the intelligence mosaic, I recommend that periphery intelligence be run on a 24/7 basis to the point that the opposition is publicly rebuking the actions of the host country. One can study the reaction times of other nations and get a sense of their command structure. The way the current intelligence community is set up cannot account for the talent of the individuals who participate in it. Intelligence agencies should all fall under two agencies: (1) original talent (creating the fundamentals of intelligence); and (2) creative talent (creating the dynamics of intelligence). An example of this: talent built the computer, and the social media site Facebook created new marketing intelligence/strategies. By May of 1962, the United States started to position naval vessels off the coast of Cuba.

17 Open-source intelligence is responsible for the gathering of literature, news, and any current events in the host country. By piecing together information from different sources, one could predict the probable actions of a country's political and military leadership. Open-source intelligence is part of that intelligence mosaic that an analyst needs; it is the ribbon on the prize, neatly wrapping up the intelligence framework one created.

18 The term for rocket in Spanish is *cohete*, a term used by the refugees. Unskilled observers can provide a plethora of information; even if it is inconsistent, it may resemble the intelligence mosaic the analyst created. During this time, Cuban refugees would report on truck activity throughout the entire Cuban island at all times of the night, as well as large-scale construction activity (Central Intelligence Agency, 1963).

19 The SA-2 is a surface-to-air missile that can reach up to speeds past [blank] with a maximum effective altitude of [blank]. The "blank" means that this is possibly classified information.

20 Secret writing through some form of snail mail is usually the most reliable piece of intelligence, but also the slowest way to disseminate information. Other agents in Cuba reported Cuban officers discussing the use of their new atomic weapons. This was confirmed in part by reports of Soviet trucks pulling long trailers carrying objects covered by canvas (Central Intelligence Agency, 1963).

indicated much more detail about Soviet activities, the agents reporting that large intercontinental rockets over 20 meters long had been unloaded from a ship docked at the Port of Mariel on September 19.[21] By October 2, a refugee schoolteacher confirmed the report at the Port of Mariel that missiles had been unloaded from Soviet ships.[22] The Kennedy administration opted for responsive military action in the form of a naval blockade of Cuba as well as a political solution to the Cuban Missile Crisis by publicly attacking the Soviets in the United Nations for the world to see what they were up to. This was a brilliant strategy for the Kennedy administration, as it illustrated how the Soviet Union was incapable of preparing for a military and political response simultaneously because its center of command is not decentralized. Therefore, information takes more time to reach the top command levels as it has to be filtered through the Politburo (administrative functions of the executive level) and then the Kremlin.

The Cuban Missile Crisis also portrayed the Soviets as adventurists willing to risk capitulation toward the West; at least that is what the Chinese thought. After the Cuban Missile Crisis, there was a split in Soviet priorities. In a November 1962 article in *Red Star*, Marshal Chuikov published a 1920 conversation between Stalin and Lenin where they stated that diplomacy weakens achieved military victories. This was an obvious hit toward Khrushchev's political power. The Soviet Union went from a stance of "must always have superiority in armed forces" to one of parity with the West. This was done to salvage hurt Soviet prestige during the Cuban Missile Crisis.[23]

Chapter 2: Identify the Following Key Players and Events

- Cuban Missile Crisis
  - Bay of Pigs Invasion
- Intelligence mosaic
  - Open-source intelligence

---

21   Not all intelligence comes to the intelligence mosaic at the same time; if you have secret writing using snail mail, your report, although important to verify other reports, may be as old as a month (Central Intelligence Agency, 1963).

22   Low-flying aircraft reported that ships were carrying jet bombers to Cuba. Photos were consistently being taken by the National Photographic Interpretation Center (NPIC) (Central Intelligence Agency, 1963).

23   Central Intelligence Agency, 1963.

- Central Intelligence Agency
  - *cohete*
- General Maxwell Taylor
  - MRBMs
- Caribbean Admission Center (CAC)
  - CIA historian Jack B. Pfeiffer
- Cuban refugees
  - Anti-Castro Cuban exiles

Discussion Questions

With the focus questions in mind, try to see the discussion questions from a neutral and objective point of view. This may be difficult at first, but it also may give new insight into the situation that was occurring during this time. More importantly, it will add a sense of reasonableness to your logical way of thinking.

1. What challenges was Khrushchev having with balancing the Soviet military and Soviet economics?
2. Why was Cuba an important asset to the Soviet Union?
3. What made President Kennedy hesitate to invade Cuba?
4. Why was it necessary to accumulate as much intelligence as possible?
5. What challenges did both the United States and the USSR have once the Cuban Missile Crisis became known to the public?

Comparative Essay

Directions: Read the following passage and write an essay that compares the actions of the United States collection of intelligence over Cuba and how President George W. Bush decided to invade Iraq because of its weapons of mass destruction program.

The Kennedy administration used deliberate intelligence-gathering methods to decide to potentially attack Cuba and remove Castro. Kennedy learned the lessons of the Bay of Pigs, not to rush into any action because it may not go as planned. President Kennedy, like most of his predecessors, followed the Monroe Doctrine, which can be summed up this way: the United States would concern itself with the affairs of the Western Hemisphere, to include Central and South America, and that there should be no interference from Russia or any foreign power. Such aggression toward the American sphere of influence could be construed as an act of war. If it is appropriate for the United States to live and even die by such a doctrine, then why is it not for other countries? How can the United States justify an invasion of Iraq while still upholding the Monroe Doctrine? Find out what intelligence-gathering evidence that Secretary of State Colin Powell presented before the UN Security Council. Was it enough to convince you?

Time Line

- 1949–1960—Germans from East Germany flood into West Germany
- 1955–1958—Khrushchev begins reducing the size of the Soviet military
- 1961 April—The Soviet Union launches a cosmonaut into space
- 1961 April—Bay of Pigs Invasion
- 1961 August—East Germans and the Soviet government begin construction of the Berlin Wall
- 1962 May—The United States positions naval vessels off the coast of Cuba
- 1962 August—U-2 mission over Cuba confirms eight SA-2 sites
- 1962 October—A refugee schoolteacher confirms the report at the Port of Mariel that missiles have been unloaded from Soviet ships
- 1962 October—Cuban Missile Crisis; President Kennedy addresses the nation

Chapter 3

Vietnam Conflict, 1955–1975

A New Challenge for America

Chapter Focus

Did the Kennedy administration and later the Johnson administration take the necessary steps to understand the political and social movements in Vietnam? Can you give any specific examples? How do you think the United States was perceived after the French government left Vietnam? Can you give any specific examples?

Although the Kennedy administration had challenges such as the Bay of Pigs and the Cuban Missile Crisis, the real obstacle was in Southeast Asia in Vietnam.[1] After the unfortunate death of President Kennedy, the newly sworn president Lyndon B. Johnson (LBJ) wasted no time in implementing a plan in Southeast Asia. The US military was already at a disadvantage, as the Vietnamese forces were already well organized and

---

1 According to Chester A. Bain's book entitled *Vietnam: The Roots of the Conflict*, the Sino-Soviet dispute affected the natural development of Vietnam by the Communists. The northern Communists formed a government called the Democratic Republic of Vietnam (DRV), organized in 1945 by Viet Minh and headed by Communist leader Ho Chi Minh. To the south of the 17th parallel was the State of Vietnam, comprised of anti-Communist Vietnamese nationalists organized by Emperor Bao Dai. The southern Communists were called the Viet Cong. The National Liberation Front and the People's Revolutionary Party (PRP) joined the Viet Cong in subverting the capitalist-backed Bao Dai government. Communists use a certain playbook; their biggest enemy is the bourgeoisie. If the Communists can convince the bourgeoisie to help them fight the colonialists, then the Communists can stage a revolution and establish Communist rule. Infiltration and subversion are the hallmarks of the Communist playbook in order to run a successful opposition operation.

battle tested by the earlier French incursion into Southeast Asia.[2] The highly organized Communist forces known as the Viet Minh were under the brilliant leadership of Ho Chi Minh.[3] By 1954, Ho Chi Minh and his Viet Minh forced a settlement between the Democratic Republic of Vietnam, controlled by Ho Chi Minh, and the State of Vietnam, controlled by Emperor Bao Dai; the conference became known as the Geneva Accords.[4] Like Korea, Vietnam was now split by an imaginary line that was only enforceable because of the presence of the French military. The illusion that the United States created in its commitment to have free elections in Vietnam was naive at best. The Communists had no intention of leaving their own country, of having a split country, or of having Bao Dai remain in power. By 1955, Premier Diem won a national referendum proclaiming himself president as the emperor Bao Dai made himself absent from Vietnam.[5] By 1956, the French forces had pulled out their remaining military units, and Premier Diem further isolated the northern Vietnamese by reiterating his power in the south. The elections mandated by the Geneva Accords created an unrealistic expectation by the Viet Minh and Diem supporters, that each side had control of its electoral votes; this eventually failed. At this point, there are two Vietnams,[6] one in the north, controlled by Ho Chi Minh, and one in the south, controlled by the Diem government. There is also another element to the

---

2   The Communist national movement that occurred in Vietnam put pressure on the US government to respond to a possible Sino-Soviet bloc. Vietnam was not only a political testing ground, it was a military testing ground for capitalists and Communists. Vietnam was the place where the real conflict was going on, although many battles occurred all over Indochina. Indochina consists of Vietnam, Laos, Cambodia, and Thailand. During the Kennedy administration, a small military assistance advisory group assisted Emperor Bao Dai and the French forces fighting there.

3   With the assistance of the Chinese government, Ho Chi Minh was able to control most of the northern and central provinces of Vietnam. The French were able to hold primarily onto Saigon in the south.

4   The Geneva Accords were comprised of the United States, France, Great Britain, the Soviet Union, China, Laos, Cambodia, and the two host entities, the Democratic Republic of Vietnam and the State of Vietnam. The French were to uphold a demarcation line along the 17th parallel.

5   There were many religious, rebellious, and criminal rivals throughout Vietnam as well as the Communists. The religious sects of the Cao Dai and Hoa Hao, the guerrilla fighters known as the Montagnards, and the criminal syndicate, Binh Xuyen.

6   "You cannot have an active insurgency within one's country. An insurgency only gets stronger and conventional troops are no match since an insurgency's tactics follow no apparent military formulation. Communists are geniuses at messaging, mainly because it is direct, appealing and offers directed change. Freedom and democracy are confusing to many cultures, it offers doubts and depends on a capitalist system that excludes many of its populace" (Peter Tsahiridis, personal notes).

politicization of Vietnam, that of the southern Vietnamese who supported the north. These Vietnamese were Vietnamese Communists known as Viet Cong.[7] President Diem started to feel the pressure brought about by the Ho Chi Minh government, so then proceeded to ask the United States for more technical and logistical advice.[8] Furthermore, the South Vietnamese people were not pleased with Diem's autocratic rule. By 1961, the Viet Cong were continuing their terrorist hold over the people of South Vietnam and their leaders.[9] In order to combat the new presence of US advisers and their logistical support for the south, the Viet Cong began constructing trails and roads from the north and then through Laos to the south to supply their military efforts. This trail was famously known as the Ho Chi Minh Trail.[10] In August of 1964, a North Vietnamese patrol boat engaged with a US destroyer in the Gulf of Tonkin. President Johnson ordered the US Navy to strike against naval bases in North Vietnam.[11] President Johnson was prepared for military action because in 1961, President Kennedy and his military adviser, General Maxwell Taylor, approved measures for more support to the South Vietnamese armed forces in the form of advisers and additional support through Army aviation, naval, and Air Force units. By 1962, in Tan Son Nhut and off the coast of Da Nang, the 57th, 8th, and 93rd light helicopter units began showing up.[12] Following combat and support units came the medical detachment of the 57th Huey helicopter ambulances.

---

7   During this time (1958–1960) in Vietnamese history, the Communists and nationalists were successful in infiltrating the Diem government in the south and in the north. The Communists and nationalists used bribery, murder, kidnappings, and sabotage. The main goal of Ho Chi Minh was to bring as many Vietnamese over to his side as possible.

8   However, according to Arthur M. Schlesinger in his book *Robert Kennedy and His Times*, direct action into Laos was never an option for President Kennedy because of the lessons learned from the Bay of Pigs Invasion.

9   President Kennedy increased forces in Vietnam. The US military by 1962 is directly training resistance groups and the southern Vietnamese military to combat northern Communist military forces.

10   The political unrest was increasing in South Vietnam to the point that President Diem and his brother Nhu were assassinated. This brought on even more instability and allowed the Viet Cong to further penetrate the southern government.

11   US Congress passes a resolution to repel attacks and protect South Vietnam.

12   According to Lieutenant General John J. Tolson in his monograph "Airmobility in Vietnam," by April 1962, a US Marine helicopter squadron arrived in Soc Trang in the Mekong Delta, then later transferred their H-34 helicopters to *Da Nang* for greater elevation support. Furthermore, in 1962 the 45th Transportation Battalion out of Fort Sill, Oklahoma, was deployed to Vietnam to include the 33rd and 81st light helicopter companies.

To further support the Army of the Republic of Vietnam, the 23rd Special Warfare Aviation Detachment with reconnaissance capabilities was sent to Vietnam.[13] Although there were many battles waging on the ground and in the air in Vietnam between American forces and Vietnamese Communists, one thorn in the side of the US military was the Thanh Hoa Bridge to quell the logistic capability of the Vietnamese.[14] The Thanh Hoa railroad and bridge system was known to the Vietnamese as Ham Ron, or the Dragon's Jaw, that was over the Song Ma River. On April 3, 1965, well over 70 aircraft proceeded, mostly from Korat Air Base toward the Dragon's Jaw with Bullpup missiles and 750-pound general purpose bombs.[15] Despite the amount of armament that the US air forces disbursed on the Ham Ron Bridge, they failed to destroy it, forcing the United States to go back the next day and try again, knowing that the enemy forces would be ready for them. No matter how many hundreds of bombs hit the bridge, it remained standing. Eventually, the air strikes caused the bridge to be out of commission, but in May of that same year the Vietnamese managed to fix the necessary parts to

---

13   According to Lieutenant General John J. Tolson in his monograph "Airmobility in Vietnam," Secretary of Defense McNamara in September of 1961 directed the military to have larger procurement numbers at a much faster rate when it came to the Bell utility helicopter program. McNamara was driven to expand land warfare options: (1) explore the opportunities offered by technology; (2) explore quantum increases in effectiveness; (3) exploit the potential of aeronautics and increase its effectiveness; and (4) reexamine the tactical mobility requirements. Replacing ground transportation strategies with air transportation strategies offers greater mobility as well as quicker response times for land warfare (Peter Tsahiridis, personal notes); however, the enemy has to worry only about two things, according to Chester A. Bain's book entitled *Vietnam, the Roots of Conflict*: Vietnamese Communists had the choice when facing off with a superior force that had a greater technical superiority: (1) stage a tactical retreat; or (2) continue the struggle at all costs. This posed a problem for the technologically advanced US forces in Vietnam. How does one gauge success over the enemy through the use of technology? All the enemy has to do is find weaknesses in US technology and exploit them. It would be difficult to judge the effectiveness of US war-fighting technology if the enemy retreats at times, then makes an all-out effort at other times. This is why it is so important for US forces to hold ground. The holding of ground then signals to the enemy to either waste the effort in attacking or to move on to a different strategy. If the United States illustrates land superiority supported by air superiority, then the enemy will gauge its penetrability and face the fact of a US presence in its country warfare (Peter Tsahiridis, personal notes).

14   ARNO Press published a book entitled *Air War Vietnam* that discusses the logistical challenges of the US air campaign.

15   According to *Air War Vietnam*, the Bullpups could be launched from 12,000 feet and the 750-pound bombs could be dropped between 4,000 and 6,000 feet. "This may become a logistical problem for the U.S. to destroy a fortified establishment only 56-feet wide. Steel and concrete fortifications remain solid depending on the angle of attack, anything more than 15-degrees will usually have no effect, furthermore, any type of wind change can affect the target being hit" (Peter Tsahiridis, personal notes).

continue railroad operations. Again, the US air forces would strike at the bridge, causing enough damage to close it for repairs, but it still remained in operation. The result of such repetitious missions caused delay and allowed the enemy time to adapt to the policies of the US military campaign.

The North Vietnamese in Hanoi feared more US airstrikes would come; therefore, Hanoi's leaders communicated their concern to the Soviet Union. In response, the Soviet Union would transport any remaining North Vietnamese aircraft by Soviet Mi-6 heavy-duty helicopters to a more obscure mountainous region away from Hanoi. In order to counter the North Vietnamese Army, the United States decided to send more combat US Army and Marines. The US military decided to control Route 19, which was between Pleiku and the Central Highlands of Qui Nhon. The most effective and quickest way to secure logical superiority on the ground was to send in the 1st Cavalry Division airmobile units. However, holding logistical lines was increasingly difficult in Vietnam as the enemy would consistently attack the long, stretched-out convoys of American vehicles. Reactions from the 3rd Marine Division and 1st Cavalry Division formidably held ground and destroyed the Viet Cong in Quan Ngi Province, while the 1st Cavalry Division destroyed North Vietnamese military divisions in the Ia Drang Valley, with the added strength of B-52 bombers exploding ordnance on Viet Cong positions. By the end of 1965, over 140,000 American soldiers were deployed in Vietnam. American supply lines through Route 19 and the continued use of the Ho Chi Minh Trail, which went through Laos and Cambodia, meant that both sides would not give up their logistical advantage. While the Communist forces of the Viet Cong and the US forces battled, chaos and instability were once again hitting South Vietnam, with the overthrow of President Diem and his ousting in 1963 to the military junta of South Vietnamese generals to the civilian government headed by Premier Nguyen Xuen Oanh, which was put in place by General Khanh. Eventually, even Khanh was ousted from power where the military government bent to the pressure of the South Vietnamese people in favor of Premier Phan Huy Quat in late February of 1965.[16] With the continuous uncertainty of the Vietnamese government, this only emboldened the Communists to pursue their goals even further. President Johnson publicly declared that the US

---

16 US National Security Adviser McGeorge Bundy briefs President Johnson on the situation in Vietnam and even advises the Johnson administration that the use of nuclear weapons may be advisable (Kifner, 1996).

and South Vietnamese governments might have to conduct air missions in North Vietnam. This is unacceptable to the Soviet Union, which immediately makes its intentions clear about US involvement in the north. Soviet premier Alexi Kosygin promises that the Soviet Union will supply military aid to the north if attacked by the United States. In order to bring about a negotiation settlement, President Lyndon Johnson continued air strikes into northern Vietnam. At this point in 1965, the main objective of the US military is to support the South Vietnamese forces and to limit the capabilities of the North Vietnamese government in their support of the Viet Cong. By March of 1965, the United States has committed to securing the area around Da Nang in order to set up air defenses for the South Vietnamese. According to the *Chicago Tribune*, March 8, 1965, over 1,400 US Marines from the 9th Marine Expeditionary Brigade land off the coast of Da Nang to secure the air base in an operation code named Operation Red Beach 2.[17] By landing combat troops in Vietnam, this signaled a strategic increase in America's wartime effort. The combination of landing combat troops in Vietnam and continuous air strikes against the Viet Cong over Binh Tuy Province assured the Johnson administration that in no way are the Viet Cong going to take over Saigon. No matter how many times US combat air forces struck at Hanoi, it only strengthened the support of the Soviet Union toward their Vietnamese comrades. From 1964 to 1967, the US military policy against the North Vietnamese was the enforcement of graduated military pressure.[18] Applying graduated military pressure focused on three goals: (1) to signal US resolve to the Communists; (2) to strengthen the morale of the South Vietnamese military; and (3) to force the north Vietnamese to spend their monies unpredictably, as a result, assuring them to come to the table to negotiate.[19] The US policy of a military offensive "progressively mounting

---

17   There were reports that Communist forces defeated South Vietnamese forces near the Da Nang air base, but took no action against the US Marines (*Chicago Tribune*, 1965). While the US Marines were landing in Da Nang, US citizens were filling up bottles with black tar and launching them on the Russian Embassy in Washington, DC.

18   US bombings of Hanoi would cease if there was a visiting dignitary from the Soviet Union in hopes that such a meeting would spur the USSR into talking down the North Vietnamese government. However, not to look weak to the United States, the North Vietnamese military would often strike at US forces at the time of Soviet visits, which would cause an immediate reaction by the Americans in reprisal attacks. https://nara-media-001.s3.amazonaws.com/arc-media/research/pentagon-papers/Pentagon-Papers-Part-IV-C-3.pdf

19   "The problem with this type of Western policy is that it is presuming the Communist type of ideology benefits from a negotiated settlement based on the premise that it can save money. Capitalist venture is hardly motivation for Communists, in fact, it proves the Communist

in scope and intensity,"[20] where the element of pressure was the objective rather than damage inflicted, never saw Hanoi waver from its commitment to the cause of driving out the enemy. By 1965, Hanoi had a great amount of control over South Vietnam; therefore, the United States had no leverage over Hanoi and could not implement negotiations. President Johnson then decided to order the bombing of North Vietnam. On March 2, 1965, a new mission named Rolling Thunder V was initiated by US combat air forces and the Republic of Vietnam Air Force (VNAF), targeting Hanoi and other Communist strategic holdings. US Secretary of State Dean Rusk signaled to the North Vietnamese that the United States would not negotiate unless Hanoi stopped its military actions to the south. Until then, the United States would continuously conduct air strikes over key Communist strategic points.[21] In essence, the United States relied on the faulty premise that by denying the North Vietnamese and the Viet Cong victory, this should be sufficient to break their will to fight.[22] What led to this predictable stalemate in 1965? There is instability in South Vietnam; South Korea sends in military troops; the civilian government in South Vietnam is ousted and the military takes over; the US Navy takes control of water routes throughout Vietnam; the Soviets expand economic and military assistance to Hanoi; the United States steps up air attacks all over the northern part of Vietnam; VC terrorists attack enlisted US soldiers; President Johnson executes operation Rolling Thunder; sustained air attacks against the North Vietnamese; the United States hits logistical railroads and bridges in North Vietnam; China puts political pressure on America to stop bombing the north part of Vietnam; Yugoslavian president Tito urges President Johnson to stop the bombings in

---

message is authentic, that the fight and struggle produced by capitalism is for leverage with the end result being negotiation, whereas the Communist ideology is based on the philosophy of how one shall live with others in equality where capitalism has minimal value" (Peter Tsahiridis, personal notes). https://nara-media-001.s3.amazonaws.com/arcmedia/research/pentagon-papers/Pentagon-Papers-Part-IV-C-3.pdf

20   https://nara-media-001.s3.amazonaws.com/arcmedia/research/pentagon-papers/Pentagon-Papers-Part-IV-C-3.pdf

21   https://nara-media-001.s3.amazonaws.com/arcmedia/research/pentagon-papers/Pentagon-Papers-Part-IV-C-3.pdf

22   This new policy was introduced by Secretary McNamara and called *interdiction*, which meant to stop something from happening; in this case, the air strikes in the north part of Vietnam. The United States would pause the air strikes to see the Communist reactions and "offer" a chance for the North Vietnamese to change their policies. This type of strategy was often met with mistrust. It clearly indicates that nations do not trust each other when one of them has leverage.

Vietnam; and the landing of two Marine battalions at Da Nang.[23] By 1967, the North Vietnamese Army (NVA) pushes south through the Ho Chi Minh Trail to engage against US ground forces; and the Viet Cong "Charlie" push toward Saigon. In response, the US military fully engages in Vietnam in the areas of the Mekong Delta, the provinces of Quang Nam, Binh Dinh, Quang Tri, Thua Thien, and Pleiku, exacting heavy casualties on the NVA and Viet Cong forces, sometimes killing thousands of enemy forces per battle. By June of 1967, there are over 450,000 US troops in Vietnam, with well over 250,000 enemy forces, including the NVA.

President Nixon, Stepping Up the Game

Weakening support for the Vietnam War in 1968 was reinforced by the Tet Offensive, in which the North Vietnamese and the Viet Cong systematically attacked all the major cities in South Vietnam; as a result, a half a million south Vietnamese were displaced, as well as creating destruction and death. The coordinated attacks by the North Vietnamese and the Viet Cong challenged US ideas of fighting in Southeast Asia, which brought on protests and presidential challenges from Democratic senators Eugene McCarthy of Minnesota and Robert Kennedy of New York, as well as from Vice President Hubert H. Humphrey. As a response to the political unrest and unpopularity of the Vietnam War, President Johnson tried to deescalate the conflict by inviting the North Vietnamese to begin peace talks in Paris by May of 1968. He also announced that he would not accept the nomination of his party for another term as president. Former politician Richard Nixon fought off the Republican candidates Governor George Romney of Michigan, Ronald Reagan of California, and Governor Nelson Rockefeller of New York to win the nomination. On June 5, 1968, after winning the California primary election for the Democratic Party, Senator Kennedy was killed by an assassin. This spawned protests and anger within the Democratic Party, where the struggle between Vice President Humphrey and Senator George McGovern of South Dakota was apparent during the Democratic

---

23 There seemed to be disagreement within the Johnson administration about air strikes. Apparently, bombing enemy targets as reprisals has limited effect and sustained bombings would have influenced the North Vietnamese more, but President Johnson would have had to take on more political pressure if he issued relentless air strikes. https://nara-media-001.s3.amazonaws.com/arcmedia/research/pentagon-papers/Pentagon-Papers-Part-IV-C-3.pdf

Convention in Chicago. There, followers for each candidate exploded into the streets of Chicago, clashing with police. This kind of instability over Vietnam fashioned an independent party to emerge under former governor George Wallace of Alabama. The invasion of Czechoslovakia in October of 1968 strengthened the Brezhnev Doctrine, which ultimately was a series of actions taken by the Soviet Union to use military force to persuade its satellite countries to follow the lead of Moscow.[24] Meanwhile, a month later, over 73 million Americans cast their vote in the 1968 election. Richard Nixon won the popular count by half a million votes and dominated the Electoral College: 302 votes for Nixon, 191 votes for Humphrey, and 43 votes for Wallace.

President Nixon tapped on the intellectual energy of Henry A. Kissinger as his national security adviser, then later put Kissinger in charge of the State Department. Kissinger realized that the old paradigm of US policy engaging against the Soviet Union or even China, based on the fact they were Communist nations, limited the negotiation strategies of the United States. Therefore, Kissinger would advise President Nixon to abandon the old policy of containment and replace it with practical considerations; meaning, if China and/or the Soviet Union's interests could profit America monetarily or strategically, then they could begin negotiating for mutual benefit. President Nixon presented his vision of the world, which included a balanced world having a strong China, Soviet Union, Europe, United States, and Japan all benefiting from cooperation rather than from fighting. The Nixon Doctrine of helping allies and friends (but ultimately giving them the responsibility to defend themselves) supported Nixon's view of a balanced world. This meant that Nixon's involvement in Vietnam would eventually shift the burden of responsibility back to the South Vietnamese government to fight its own battles. The intent was to keep the Thieu regime in Saigon and negotiate a peace with the Ho Chi Minh government in Hanoi. As the talks in Paris collapsed over the issue of peace in Vietnam, President Nixon addressed American citizens in a televised speech stating that the silent majority of Americans believe in the fight over Vietnam. This message had the same effect of building a wall between the American people, those who opposed the war and those who supported it. Nixon pushed for the Vietnamization of the war, meaning training and supporting South Vietnamese troops as the American forces of over 500,000 withdrew. However, Nixon's

---

24 White, 2016.

promise to remove American troops and reduce American involvement from Vietnam took another turn when in late April of 1970, Nixon ordered the US military and South Vietnamese forces to invade the neutral country of Cambodia to take out Communist forces of the North Vietnamese. The bombing of Cambodia ended in June 1970. By February 1971, Nixon ordered an invasion of Laos by giving air support to the South Vietnamese ground forces; unlike in Cambodia, US ground forces were restricted by the Congress in the Defense Appropriations Act of 1970.[25] In January of 1972, Nixon promised the American people that the American forces in Vietnam would be reduced to 69,000; yet even that comforting announcement did not stop the level of violence in Vietnam or the increase of US military casualties and the political and social unrest in America. Although troop withdrawals were underway, President Nixon stepped up the naval and air campaigns, dropping more bombs over Vietnam targeting North Vietnamese Communists.

China, the Other Power

Although China was a superpower, it remained relatively neutral in its stance supporting Communist causes and often separated itself from the Soviet Union. The increase in status of the Chinese as a superpower stems from the fact that the Chinese tested their first atomic bomb in 1964 and first hydrogen bomb in 1967.[26] To help ease the relations between the People's Republic of China and the U.S. in 1971, the UN admitted the People's Republic of China and dismissed nationalist China (Taiwan) from a seat on the Security Council.[27] By February of 1972, President Nixon was in China as a visiting dignitary and participating in summit meetings, which resulted in Beijing and Washington, DC developing trade agreements. Although

---

25 Congress in the Defense Appropriations Act of 1970, according to the Congressional Research Service: "U.S. ground troops withdrew by June 30, 1970, but U.S. bombing of North Vietnamese and Khmer Rouge forces in Cambodia continued. Proposed and enacted amendments in Congress were designed to prohibit both the reintroduction of U.S. ground forces into Cambodia after June 30, 1970 and continued U.S. aerial bombing of Cambodia. The 'Cooper-Church' amendment, enacted into law in January 1971, prohibited the reintroduction of U.S. ground forces into Cambodia. The restrictive bills passed in June and July 1973 mandated an end to the bombing in Cambodia by August 15, 1973, and bombing stopped on that date" (Belasco, 2007).

26 China tests its first atomic and hydrogen bombs in the 1960s.

27 China is admitted to the UN Security Council (Lei, 2014).

promising, the agreements between Beijing and Washington, DC did not overshadow the fact that China was frustrated that Taiwan had an embassy in the United States. This one factor bothered Communist China to the point that they refused to help America in the Vietnam War. By 1973, the Nixon administration agreed to move American forces out of Taiwan to help in the developing relationship with Beijing.[28] Although the United States was deescalating the number of troops, missions, and monies to Vietnam, President Nixon could not escape the political chaos within his own administration, and on August 8, 1974, he resigned from office. This was a signal to the Communists, the Khmer Rouge army of Cambodia, and the North Vietnamese forces, who committed themselves to an all-out attack on Vietnam, capturing Phuoc Long Province, attacking Ban Me Thuot, Quan Tri City, Quang Ngail City, the US Marine base at Chu Lai, Da Nang air base, and Phnom Penh in Cambodia, causing the evacuation of Saigon. By April 1975, the Communists captured Saigon and renamed it Ho Chi Minh City. The ultimate lesson of Vietnam is to not underestimate the importance of why other cultures fight for a cause. To understand the cause of the other gives one a better idea of what can inflict harm on the enemy. The US government never understood this concept. US leadership only understood technological advancement, costs, and analysis, while the enemy understood that to defeat a superior enemy, one must be united in an idea. That idea was to free Vietnam from its invaders.

Chapter 3: Identify the Following Key Players and Events

- President Johnson
  - President Nixon
- Viet Cong
  - Rolling Thunder
- Pentagon Papers
  - Brezhnev
- North Vietnamese Army (NVA)
  - US Secretary of State Dean Rusk
- Ho Chi Minh Trail
  - General Khanh

---

28 Nixon removes American troops from Taiwan (U.S. Secretary of State, 2017).

- General Maxwell Taylor
  - Ho Chi Minh

Discussion Questions

1. What tactics did the Viet Cong use to sabotage the South Vietnamese government under Diem's rule?
2. What sorts of challenges did President Johnson have in Vietnam that President Kennedy did not?
3. What was so significant about the Tet Offensive?
4. What type of leader was Leonid Brezhnev?
5. What type of message was Hanoi sending to the United States and the South Vietnamese?

Comparative Essay

Directions: Read the following passage and write an essay that compares the strengths and weaknesses of détente in the context of assessing Richard Nixon's presidency.

Détente (1971–1972) was the US foreign policy of the easing of hostility or strained relations with the Soviet Union. Since the Vietnam War, both the United States and the Soviet Union had policies that only antagonized each other. The cost of the Vietnam War was devastating to America. Investigate President Nixon's domestic policies. Would any of these domestic policies (the war on poverty, the Clean Air Act, Nixon's health care plan to low-income families, the opening of China, and the advancement of women in the workforce) been possible without détente? Visit the websites www .nixonlibrary.gov/forresearchers/index.php and explore the life of Richard Nixon as president and www.nixonlibrary.gov/virtuallibrary/index.php and view the many documents and recorded tapes by Nixon. Focus on the relationship between Nixon's presidency and his engagement with the Soviet Union. Was President Nixon taking the right path toward fighting Communism? How was Nixon's path different from his predecessors?

Time Line

- 1964 April—Gulf of Tonkin incident with enemy Vietnamese patrol boats engaging the US destroyers USS *Maddox* and USS *C. Turner Joy*
- 1964 October—US Special Forces commit support to South Vietnam forming an alternative government throughout the countryside
- 1965 January—The South Korean government sends military advisers to South Vietnam to support the mission
- 1965 February—The Soviet Union announces it will provide military aid to North Vietnam
- 1965 March—Soviet participation on the side of North Vietnam
- 1965 March—The US Embassy in Saigon is attacked by exploding bombs
- 1965 May—The Soviet Union deploys SA-2 missiles around Hanoi to beef up its defenses
- 1965 June—The United States deploys troops along with South Vietnamese military units
- 1965 July—President Johnson initiates sending more US combat troops to Vietnam, raising the number from 75,000 troops to 125,000

Chapter 4

The Carter Administration, 1977–1981

What Is Tangible and What Is Achievable

Chapter Focus

Was President Carter's lack of experience in foreign affairs detrimental to challenging the Communist threat? Can you give any specific examples? How had the fight against Communism changed since the terms of President Johnson and President Nixon? Can you give any specific examples?

"I assume the Presidency under extraordinary circumstances. ... This is an hour of history that troubles our minds and hurts our hearts."
—*President Gerald Ford*[1]

S oviet relations during the Ford presidency were characterized by the fact that both sides had a healthy and honest respect for one another. Both sides preserved the line within the détente agreement.[2] The political reality was that President Ford lost to former Governor of Georgia Jimmy

---

1 https://www.whitehouse.gov/about-the-white-house/presidents/gerald-r-ford/

2 https://www.cia.gov/library/readingroom/docs/DOC_0000307809.pdf According to the CIA, in 1971, two-way trade amounted to $220 million and trade between the Soviet Union and the United States possibly increased under détente. The Soviets needed aluminum oxide, cattle hides, ore mining equipment, feed-grains, motor vehicle equipment, machine tools, gas pipeline equipment, and electronics. The point is that the United States never stopped trading with the Soviet Union. There is ideological policy, and there is trade. They must be separated when conducting diplomacy.

Carter on November 2, 1976. Americans were tired of the distresses of the Vietnam War and the Watergate scandal under President Nixon. Jimmy Carter won the election with 297 electoral votes to President's Ford's 240 electoral votes.[3]

The Carter administration was coming into foreign policy based on the Ford administration's adoption of the Helsinki Final Act on August 1, 1975. There were three baskets that the Helsinki Act covered: military issues, economics, and human rights.[4] The Carter administration focused on the issue of human rights, based upon the recommendation of the new National Security Advisor, Zbigniew Brzezinski, who knew that the Soviet Union would not know how to solve its human rights problem, thus allowing for a multifaceted alliance between the European allies and any resistance that was building up in Eastern Europe. The people caught in the Soviet bloc could now report the activities of the Soviet military to international onlookers because of the direct approach to human rights that President Carter took. President Carter and National Security Advisor Brzezinski withdrew from previous administrations' stance of creating power blocs and spheres of influence, moving toward things that were tangible and achievable. Former Soviet scientist Andrei Sakharov, on his acceptance speech for his Nobel Peace Prize in 1975, stated his support for human rights and peace.[5] Other notable dissidents, like Czech playwright Vaclav Havel[6] and former Soviet Vladimir Bukovsky[7], were strong advocates for human rights. The Carter administration, under the guidance of Brzezinski, obviously hit the right mark against the Soviets; the notion of human rights was beneath the Soviets, a soft issue only they were privileged to fix.

The Soviets had no answer to the human rights problem, as was evident in the May 7, 1977, incident with Stanislaw Pyjas, who was found beaten

---

3   It came as a surprise that Jimmy Carter, an outsider, won the election. The key question to ask is whether this upsets US–Soviet relations. Under President Ford there was good momentum to continue talks about peace and a desire to increase trade. How will Jimmy Carter be perceived by the Soviets?

4   https://history.state.gov/milestones/1969-1976/helsinki

5   https://www.nobelprize.org/nobel_prizes/peace/laureates/1975/sakharov-acceptance.html

6   https://www.nytimes.com/2011/12/19/world/europe/vaclav-havel-dissident-playwright-who-led-czechoslovakia-dead-at-75.html Vaclav Havel was one of the leading voices for freedom and the dismantling of Communism in the Soviet Union. He later served as the Czech Republic's president.

7   https://www.cato.org/people/vladimir-bukovsky An advocate for the reform of the Soviet Union and later reform of Russia.

to death in Krakow. Pyjas was a member of the anticommunist student movement, and his death, which was ruled an accident, did not sit well with the Polish community.[8] As a result of Pyjas' death, student activists became more aware of the sadistic nature of the State Security Service in Poland. Brzezinski's focus on human rights was now taking affect all over the Soviet bloc countries. With the Soviet Union invading Hungary in 1956, Czechoslovakia in 1968, and Afghanistan in 1979, the Carter administration had plenty of ammunition to attack Soviet General Secretary Brezhnev's idea of the perfect Soviet society. Brzezinski knew that factions throughout Eastern Europe and the rest of the world would start to resist the spread of the Communist ideas of the Soviets. How important a role did the issue of human rights play when shaping global power structures?

Marxists seized power in Kabul, Afghanistan, in 1978, and by December 1979, intelligence reports came in about a Soviet military buildup near the Soviet-Afghanistan border near the Amu Dara River. By December 25, a Soviet army of about 100,000 men crossed into Afghanistan.[9] By not willing to risk the loss of Communist control over Afghanistan, the USSR paid little attention to the risks involved when conquering this territory.[10] The Soviet methods of control over its geographic neighbors was dubbed the Brezhnev Doctrine.[11] By 1978, the president's assistant for national security affairs, Zbigniew Brzezinski, had to make a decision whether to recognize the new power in Afghanistan or not.[12]

The Soviet invasion of Afghanistan in 1979 prompted President Jimmy Carter to give this address during his 1980 State of the Union, in part:

> But now the Soviet Union has taken a radical and an aggressive new step. It's using its great military power against a relatively defenseless nation. The implications of the Soviet invasion of Afghanistan could

---

8   https://nekropole.info/en/Stanislaw-Pyjas

9   Nancy Peabody Newell and Richard S. Newell's book *The Struggle for Afghanistan* is a must-read for anyone interested in the plight of the Afghani people.

10   "There is always a problem for the invading country, in this case, the USSR, it is more difficult to retreat or give up ground" (Peter Tsahiridis, personal notes). The Soviets spent millions of dollars economically to keep a relationship with the Afghanistan government, according to Nancy Peabody Newell and Richard S. Newell.

11   The Brezhnev Doctrine states basically that once a nation or government becomes Socialist, the Soviets would keep it that way so it never goes back to capitalism.

12   (The Real News, 2017) interview with Zbigniew Brzezinski.

pose the most serious threat to the peace since the Second World War. ... While this invasion continues, we and the other nations of the world cannot conduct business as usual with the Soviet Union. That's why the United States has imposed stiff economic penalties on the Soviet Union. I will not issue any permits for Soviet ships to fish in the coastal waters of the United States. I've cut Soviet access to high-technology equipment and to agricultural products. I've limited other commerce with the Soviet Union, and I've asked our allies and friends to join with us in restraining their own trade with the Soviets and not to replace our own embargoed items. And I have notified the Olympic Committee that with Soviet invading forces in Afghanistan, neither the American people nor I will support sending an Olympic team to Moscow.[13]

The Soviet military was bogged down in Afghanistan for over nine years. The Afghani resistance fighters adapted to Soviet aggression, changed their tactics, and adopted Western-style fighting tactics. Read the following article by Patrick G. v entitled *Zbigniew Brzezinski and the Helsinki Final Act*. Vaughan points out that the Carter administration had to face many challenges under Brezhnev, challenges that ran contrary to prior US foreign policy. Look for the nuances that differentiate the ideas of Brzezinski with those of Henry Kissinger. Why was the softer approach the better approach when dealing with the Soviets?

---

13   In President Jimmy Carter's 1980 State of the Union address, he condemned the actions of the Soviet Union in Afghanistan; this was President Carter's attempt to punish the Soviet Union politically and economically (Jimmy Carter State of the Union, 1980).

Zbigniew Brzezinski and the Helsinki Final Act

Patrick G. Vaughan

On the morning of October 5, 1976 Zbigniew Brzezinski sat across from Jimmy Carter in a suite at the St Francis Hotel in San Francisco. Carter had summoned his primary foreign policy adviser to prepare for that evening's debate with President Gerald Ford. Carter, barefoot and in blue jeans, was not in a good mood. He had left the Democratic convention in July leading Ford with the largest margin recorded in modern polling. But the Ford campaign had pulled the race even, largely by hammering away at the point that Carter lacked the necessary experience in foreign affairs.

This added an even greater importance to that evening's debate dealing with foreign affairs. A satellite hookup had broadened the audience to some 300 million people around the world, the largest television audience since Neil Armstrong stepped foot on the moon.[1] Carter, widely known as a foreign policy novice, would also be debating Henry Kissinger, Ford's Secretary of State, and chief foreign policy adviser since he inherited the White House from Richard Nixon in August of 1974.

Brzezinski was known as among the more vocal critics of Henry Kissinger's version of détente with the Soviet Union. Indeed, that morning newspapers were portraying the Carter–Ford debate as a proxy war between their two high profile advisers.

Brzezinski believed the Helsinki Final Act was a key toward a more 'reciprocal' version of détente with the Soviet Union. Brzezinski, writing in the late 1960s, repeatedly urged the United States to take the lead in a major European-wide conference. This was hardly conventional wisdom. It was the Soviet leadership, not the United States, that had begun calling for such a conference since the 1960s.

---

1 'The Debates,' *Newsweek*, September 27, 1976, p. 24.

Patrick G. Vaughan, "Zbigniew Brzezinski and the Helsinki Final Act," *The Crisis of Détente in Europe: From Helsinki to Gorbachev, 1975-1985*, ed. Leopoldo Nuti, pp. 11-25. Copyright © 2009 by Taylor & Francis Group. Reprinted with permission.

They had done so, it was thought, in order to gain Western acceptance over the Soviet conquest over Eastern Europe and the Baltic states of Latvia, Estonia and Lithuania.

Brzezinski countered that a conference would be in the US interest, moving the debate away from a 'static' détente with Moscow, and toward the grander aim of ending the civil war within the developed world. Brzezinski noted,

> A European Security Conference could be a desirable step in that direction. We should think of it as a process, the purpose of which is to explore and only eventually resolve the various outstanding legacies of World War II but we will not be able to do so if the West— and particularly the United States—keeps shrinking away from the challenge on the jejune argument that we can't enter a conference unless we know in advance what its outcome will be.[2]

Nixon and Kissinger saw little advantage in opening up a multilateral European framework while engaged in a bilateral détente with Moscow. Yet, as a side note to the 1972 summit in Moscow, Nixon agreed to a European Security Conference.

Deliberations on the Conference on Security and Cooperation (CSCE) began in Helsinki on November 22, 1972.[3] It was the West European nations that most actively promoted the idea of increasing human contacts and insisting on freer flows of information toward the Soviet Union and Eastern Europe, later known in the CSCE lexicon as the 'Basket Three' proposals. The United States representation, in stark contrast, stressed the need for greater 'realism' and sought to 'reign in' the Western Europeans from dwelling on such potentially destabilizing issues such as human rights.[4]

Kissinger's dismissal of the European approach was seen at a NATO meeting in June 1974, when he quipped that the Soviet system had 'survived for fifty years' and 'would not be changed if Western newspapers were put on sale in a few kiosks in Moscow.'[5]

> 'I do not think,' said a member of a West European delegation of Kissinger, 'he understands the genuinely idealistic elements in the

2   Z. Brzezinski, 'Détente in the 70s,' *The New Republic*, January 3, 1970, p. 18.

3   For an early look at the CSCE's impact on Eastern Europe see A. Bromke, 'The CSCE and Eastern Europe,' *The World Today*, vol. 29 no. 5, May 1973, pp. 202–3.

4   B. Kovrig, *Of Walls and Bridges: The United States and Eastern Europe*, New York: New York University Press, 1991, p. 168.

5   D. C. Thomas, *The Helsinki Effect: International Norms, Human Rights, and the Demise of Communism*, Princeton: Princeton University Press, 2001, p. 78.

European approach but rather, in the manner of his hero Metternich, wants stability and détente (in the Russian sense of the word) for their own sakes.'[6]

Brzezinski had begun to take a more critical view of the Nixon–Kissinger détente.

> While the Soviet side has continued to proclaim domestically that the ideological conflict must go on unabated and that therefore severe restrictions of basic human rights are justified, the US side has been relatively inactive at the East–West European Conference now in progress, where the West Europeans have been assertively demanding freer East–West contacts, and it has been quietly reducing the effectiveness of both Radio Free Europe and Radio Liberty, which for less than 15 cents per head per year have become the most significant US levers for freer communications—and thus for social change—in Eastern Europe and the Soviet Union.[7]

By early 1976 Jimmy Carter had emerged as the unlikely front runner for the Democratic nomination. All foreign policy memos had to pass through Brzezinski. Any staff member who tried to give a memo directly to Carter was met with a hand wave instruction to 'clear it with Zbig.'[8] Henceforth Carter's foreign policy speeches—denouncing the 'Nixon–Ford–Kissinger obsession with power blocs and spheres of influence'—were lifted from Brzezinski's scholarly articles and campaign memos.[9] 'Hearing Brzezinski's snide words slung at him each day,' noted, Kissinger biographer, Walter Isaacson, 'not with a slightly embittered Polish accent but a smiling Georgia accent, drove Kissinger to near distraction.'[10]

The Helsinki Final Act was made public in June of 1975. The Soviet Union immediately portrayed it as a triumph of Soviet diplomacy. American conservatives denounced it as 'Yalta II.' There were some Soviet officials who expressed concerns that the 'Basket Three' sections could become a significant problem. Both Brezhnev and Foreign Minister Gromyko countered that they could go ahead and sign the Final Act, and then simply ignore the clauses they objected to. 'We

---

6   D. C. Thomas, op. cit., p. 79.

7   Z. Brzezinski, 'The Deceptive Structure of Peace,' *Foreign Policy*, vol. 14, Spring 1974, p. 42.

8   R. Sheer, 'In Search of Brzezinski,' *Washington Post*, February 6, 1977.

9   Z. Brzezinski, *Power and Principle: Memoirs of the National Security Adviser, 1977–1981*, New York: Farrar, Straus, Giroux, 1983, p. 5.

10   W. Isaacson, *Kissinger: A Biography*, New York: Simon & Schuster, 1992, p. 700.

are masters in our own house,' said Brezhnev, 'and we shall decide what we implement and what we ignore.'[11] This was, Brzezinski believed, a reasonable assumption as long as President Ford permitted Kissinger to determine the meaning of the Helsinki Final Act.

The Final Act was signed in Helsinki on August 1, 1975. The 35 representatives sat shoulder to shoulder for a silent 17 minutes as each man signed the pages in the ceremonial green-leather bound document.[12] The conference was marked by three days of speech making about what the Final Act 'really' meant. Brezhnev, increasingly frail and visibly ailing, was nevertheless firm in articulating the Soviet viewpoint. The Soviet leader, noticeably slurring during his speech, sharply enunciated his words when it came to the question of human rights. The 'main conclusion' of the conference, insisted a suddenly defiant Brezhnev, was that no one should try to dictate to others how 'they ought to manage their internal affairs.'[13]

Zbigniew Brzezinski was one of the few 'hardliners' in the United States who did not interpret Helsinki as a second Yalta. The Final Act, he believed, had codified two vital aspects of his 'peaceful engagement' program he had outlined for John Kennedy in the late 1950s. First, said Brzezinski, the Helsinki accords finalized the long disputed German–Polish border. This would finally put to rest the bogey of West German *revanschism* that Moscow had long used to legitimize its dominion over Eastern Europe. More importantly, said Brzezinski, the Helsinki accords legitimized Western concern for citizens within the Soviet Union and Eastern European states. 'The fundamental difference between Yalta and Helsinki,' Brzezinski noted later, 'was that Helsinki focused on the tangible and the achievable; Yalta was rhetorically on the high ground but in effect it was a testimony to Western weakness and shallowness.'[14]

Brzezinski, utilizing his connections at Radio Free Europe, sought to refashion the debate over the meaning of Helsinki. The 'Basket Three' section of the Final Act had given citizens the right to simply ask their oppressive communist regimes to abide by their own constitutions—and the agreements they had signed at Helsinki.

---

11   Quite an interesting omission! Where did you get Brezhnev's remark?

12   'Ford's Big Gamble on Détente,' *Newsweek*, August 4, 1975, p. 16.

13   J. F. Clarity, 'Soviet Wary of the Internal Effects of Détente Abroad,' *New York Times*, August 2, 1975.

14   Z. Brzezinski, 'On Anniversaries in 1985,' *Problems of Communism*, March–April 1985, p. 88.

Bronislaw Geremek, later a key member of Solidarity, recalled Brzezinski's role as crucial in changing the debate over the perception of the Helsinki Final Act.

> To say very frankly we in the Polish opposition had some serious doubts about the Helsinki process. We initially thought it was another situation where the Russians were superior negotiators to the Western politicians, as expressed by Lenin when he said the West would 'produce the rope that would hang themselves.' It was thus extremely important to us that Zbigniew Brzezinski was involved in the process and that he supported Basket Three. The dissidents, until this time, had this feeling of being marginal, and had no legal reference. But with the Helsinki agreement, and especially this 'third basket,' we could say to our government: 'You signed it—if you signed the agreement, we are now asking about the agreements on freedom of information, freedom of expression, travels and so on.' So Brzezinski's role in emphasizing the third basket was crucial, and this, I have no doubt, played a key role in the implosion of the Soviet empire.[15]

The term 'Basket Three' gained currency in the United States only when Brzezinski began to advise Jimmy Carter to focus on it in his 1976 presidential campaign.[16] Brzezinski began to advise Carter to avoid Reagan's wholesale condemnation of the Helsinki Final Act, and instead focus on the still little known 'Basket Three' aspects that committed all signatories to respect 'civil, economic, social, cultural, and other rights and freedoms.' 'I really felt these systems were in decay and artificial,' recalled Brzezinski.

> 'So Basket Three gave us (the Carter campaign) a real opportunity to press them at the point of greater vulnerability to them, and to do it in a manner which at the same time didn't make us look as if we were just some sort of crude anti-communists interested in inflaming or re-flaming the Cold War. Carter was killing the Soviets with kindness because he was talking about engagement, human rights,

---

15   Interview with Bronislaw Geremek, May 13, 2002, Warsaw, Poland.

16   See E. Drew, 'A Reporter at Large: Human Rights,' *The New Yorker*, July 18, 1977, p. 37.

disarmament. But the Soviets knew what he was talking about it,' Brzezinski recalled, 'or at least they knew what I was thinking about.'[17]

On August 1, 1976, the one-year anniversary of the signing of the Helsinki Accords, Moscow was still commemorating the Final Act as a ringing triumph for Soviet diplomacy in special television programs and full page spreads in Soviet newspapers.[18] This was the widely shared view of the Helsinki Final Act when Brzezinski sat down with Jimmy Carter to prepare for his debate with Gerald Ford in San Francisco. Brzezinski, briefing Carter for two hours over breakfast, told the challenger he must take the initiative. 'Only by putting Ford on the defensive,' Brzezinski insisted, could Carter 'shatter the advantage of presidential incumbency.' But the key to the debate was the emphasis on 'Basket Three' of the Helsinki Final Act.

'Do not attack the Agreement as a whole,' read Brzezinski's memo.

> The so-called 'Basket III' gives us the right—for the first time—to insist on respect for human rights without this constituting interference in the internal affairs of communist states. Accordingly, this is a considerable asset for us, and you should hammer away at the proposition that the Republicans have been indifferent to this opportunity. The Helsinki Agreement also provides for the permanence of existing borders in Europe, and this happens to be in our interest. Insecurity about borders tended to drive the East Europeans (notably the Czechs and Poles) into Soviet hands. Thus, it is not in your interest to suggest that it would have been better if we had not accepted the existing borders.[19]

Brzezinski's memo also prepared a dummy answer for Carter to address any question pertaining to Eastern Europe, a question he warned was likely to come from panelist Max Frankel, a former Moscow correspondent from the New York Times: Ford, after

---

17 Interview with Zbigniew Brzezinski, March 29, 2000, Washington, DC.

18 'Taking the Measure of Helsinki,' *Time*, August 9, 1976. 'A Year After Helsinki: Despite Moscow's Promises, No Greater Freedom for East Europe,' *US News and World Report*, August 9, 1976.

19 Personal Archives, Office of Zbigniew Brzezinski, Center of Strategic and International Studies, Washington, DC, 'Points to Bear in Mind on East–West Relations,' memo dated October 1976—written by Zbigniew Brzezinski for presidential candidate Jimmy Carter.

a series of mock debates with Henry Kissinger and Brent Scowcroft, was said to be ready for any questions that might emerge dealing with Eastern Europe.

Panelist Max Frankel, as Brzezinski had predicted, challenged Ford to defend his foreign policy of détente.[20] Ford seemed eager to meet the challenge. Yet in his convoluted defense of the Helsinki Final Act, he entered the annals of debate history with his claim that 'There is no Soviet domination of Eastern Europe, and there never will be under a Ford administration.' It was a stunning statement. James Naughton of the New York Times, observed an 'audible intake of air' throughout the crowd. Brent Scowcroft, watching off the stage, was said to have 'gone white.' The debate gaffe proved a disaster for the Ford campaign. Republican hopes of exposing Carter's foreign policy 'inexperience' were dashed.

On November 2, 1976, Jimmy Carter defeated Gerald Ford in one of the closest elections in American history. Shortly thereafter, on December 18, 1976 President-elect Carter introduced Brzezinski as his new National Security Adviser in a muddy press field in Plains, Georgia. Brzezinski faced the inevitable question. 'Mr Brzezinski,' one reporter asked inevitably, 'is Secretary Kissinger going to be a tough act to follow?' Brzezinski replied 'I will let you make that judgment a number of years from now.'[21]

Brzezinski's version of détente would indeed be different than that practiced by Henry Kissinger. The Carter transition saw two opposition groups emerge in Czechoslovakia and Poland that formed the nascent foundations of the revolutions that would topple communist rule in 1989. In both cases, Brzezinski's emphasis on Basket Three of the Helsinki Final Act would prove essential.

> 'In the eyes of the Czechs and Slovaks,' said one scholar, 'the Helsinki Final Act amounted to a *post facto* condemnation of the Soviet invasion of their country; in the eyes of the Poles, the act reduced the chances of a Soviet invasion of Poland. The Carter administration's early pronouncements about human rights further heartened both peoples.'[22]

On January 1, 1977, the 'Charter 77' movement emerged in Czechoslovakia with a 3,000-word petition protesting the repressive nature of the government. In Poland

---

20   See 'Transcript of Foreign Affairs Debate Between Ford and Carter,' *New York Times*, October 7, 1976.

21   'Zbigniew Brzezinski,' *New York Times*, December 19, 1976.

22   A. Bromke, 'Czechoslovakia 1968—Poland 1978: A Dilemma for Moscow,' *International Journal*, Autumn 1978, p. 22.

an opposition group known as *KOR* (Committee for Workers' Defence) emerged following the riots of the summer of 1976. It would form the foundation of the Solidarity movement that would, before Carter left office, change the face of the twentieth century. Adam Michnik regarded Brzezinski's support of Helsinki as a turning point for the Polish opposition.

> 'Nixon and Kissinger,' said Michnik, 'had a vision like Metternich. That is "we divide the world into spheres of influence and we talk with governments." But Brzezinski understood what hardly anybody could understand at that time in America—that an ideological confrontation with the Soviet bloc had to be undertaken, and the American slogan should be "human rights".'[23]

Brzezinski hoped to make this clear in the section he contributed to Carter's inaugural speech.

> 'We are a proudly idealistic nation,' said Carter in a 14-minute speech on January 20, 1977. 'But let no one confuse our idealism with weakness. Because we are free we can never be indifferent to the fate of freedom elsewhere. Our moral sense dictates a clear cut preference for those societies which share with us an abiding respect for individual human rights.'[24]

Andrei Sakharov, the noted Soviet physicist and harsh critic of the Nixon–Kissinger détente, sensed a new era had arrived in Washington. 'For the first time,' Sakharov wrote in his memoirs, 'the head of a great power had announced an unambiguous commitment to the international defense of human rights.'[25] Sakharov quickly sent a letter addressed to Carter, expressing his appreciation for the gesture.

Carter sought Brzezinski's counsel on how to respond to Sakharov's gesture. Brzezinski had been critical of Kissinger's recommendation that President Ford did not see Alexander Solzhenitsyn when the Russian chronicler of the Soviet gulag visited Washington in 1975. Brzezinski thus advised Carter to send a polite letter

---

23 Interview Adam Michnik, March 30, 2001, Warsaw, Poland.

24 'In Changing Times, Eternal Principles,' *New York Times*, January 21, 1977.

25 See M. Scammell, 'The Prophet and the Wilderness: How the Idea of Human Rights Crippled Communism,' *The New Republic*, February 25, 1991, p. 35.

to the Soviet Union's other leading dissident assuring him that the US was not indifferent to the cause of human rights.

Carter's response to Sakharov set off a political firestorm in Washington. The new US President, it was said, had violated the unwritten 'code of détente.' Brzezinski, disturbed that the gesture even had to be rationalized, did his best. 'There was nothing inadvertent about the Carter letter,' Brzezinski told Reston. 'It was thought through, and discussed with the responsible officials at the NSC and the State Department before the President made his "prudential response".'[26]

Brzezinski later expounded his frustration in having to defend the gesture at all.

> 'Let's put all this in its proper context,' Brzezinski argued later. 'Shortly after the inauguration, the President received a letter of congratulations from the Nobel Prize Winner—to which the President decided to respond. If he had received a similar letter from a resident of say, Pinochet's Chile, every liberal in the world would have condemned him for not responding. It seemed the normal and civil thing to write a polite answer, which the President did. Besides, not to have done so would have been an act of cowardice, matching President Ford's unwillingness to see Solzhenitzyn.'[27]

The Carter Administration also spoke out in support of the nascent Charter 77 movement in Czechoslovakia. The signatories had come under relentless harassment by Czech authorities. The party-controlled press vilified the Chartists as 'Zionists' and 'cosmopolitans', 'enemies, traitors, vermin, scum' and 'agents of imperialism.' 'Those who lie on the rails to stop the train of history,' warned official pronouncements, 'must expect to get their legs cut off.' On January 14, 1977, Vaclav Havel, a noted playwright and prominent Charter 77 spokesman, was arrested by the authorities. For the next four years he would spend most of his time in prison. This was a test of whether the Carter Administration was going to move beyond the Nixon–Kissinger 'code of détente' and support human rights in the Warsaw Pact nations. Zdenek Mlynar, who had been a supporter of Dubcek's more humane brand of socialism, argued that the Western democracies had to decide whether they would allow 'supporters of internationally accepted pacts on human

---

26   Ibid.

27   G. Urban, 'A Long Conversation with Dr Zbigniew Brzezinski,' *Encounter*, 1981, p. 22.

and civil rights in Czechoslovakia to be brutally suppressed for the second time in a decade.'[28]

Brzezinski, who had been a firm critic of Lyndon Johnson's indifferent approach to Alexander Dubcek's 'Prague Spring' of 1968, thought it vital the Administration speak out in support of the Charter 77 movement. On January 26, the State Department publicly reprimanded the Czechoslovakian government for its treatment of the signatories of Charter 77. This marked the first time the State Department had publicly accused a government of failing to comply with the 1975 Helsinki Accords.[29]

The Soviet authorities moved to crack down on the founders of the Helsinki Watch Group. In early February Alexander Ginzburg, who had been administering a $365,000 fund set up by Alexander Solzhenitsyn to assist political prisoners and their families, was seized from a public phone and hauled away to a prison in the city of Kaluga, 90 miles southwest of Moscow. The next week police broke the door down and ransacked Yuri Orlov's apartment, arresting him while confiscating documents he had collected on Soviet mistreatment of political prisoners, religious groups and ethnic minorities.[30] In late February, Carter met with Vladimir Bukovsky, an expatriate Soviet dissident who had spent the majority of his life in the Soviet gulag, most recently after having been arrested after sending abroad official documents demonstrating that Soviet authorities were placing dissidents into psychiatric hospitals. Soviet officials launched an emotional campaign in an attempt to dissuade Carter from meeting Bukovsky, deriding him as 'scum' and an 'anti-Soviet criminal.'[31]

Carter received Bukovsky at the White House and assured him that the United States' support of human rights was 'permanent.' As Carter was greeting Bukovsky a group of dissenters gathered in the apartment of Yuri Orlov, the recently arrested founder of Helsinki Watch. Valentin Turchin, head of the Moscow chapter of Amnesty International, said Carter's willingness to meet Bukovsky had 'historic

28   M. Ketler, 'Prague Goes Public on Arrests,' *Washington Post* January 18, 1977.

29   B. Gwertzman, 'US Asserts Prague Violates Covenants about Human Rights,' *New York Times*, January 27, 1977.

30   'Dual Messages from Washington,' *Time*, February 14, 1977, p. 30.

31   'Moscow Hints Carter Should Snub Bukovsky,' *Washington Post*, February 25, 1977. 'Moscow's Expert on US Asserts Rights Issue May Cloud Arms Talk,' *New York Times*, March 17, 1977.

significance' and marked a dramatic reaffirmation of the United States' support for human rights.[32]

The West European governments, who had taken the heroic lead during the CSCE process, were becoming less enthralled with Carter's human rights campaign.[33] The West German government had refused to meet with Soviet dissident Andrei Amalrik, who had sought to meet with Bonn officials to discuss the recent repression of Soviet intellectuals.[34] The French government rejected a similar request from Amalrik, with the declaration that Paris would continue its 'pragmatic' policy of not defending political dissidents in other countries.[35]

In March of 1977 Secretary of State Cyrus Vance traveled to Moscow, where the Soviet Union summarily rejected outwardly the US 'deep cut' Strategic Arms Limitation Talks (SALT) proposals.[36] In a tense press conference Soviet Foreign Minister Andrei Gromyko noted that Carter's human rights policies had impacted the SALT discussions and generally 'poisoned the atmosphere' of US–Soviet relations.[37]

The following week Vance gave a prominent speech arguing that the Administration's human rights campaign must be conducted 'less stridently.' The issues concerning human rights in the Warsaw Pact countries, suggested Vance, should be pushed through private diplomatic channels whenever that approach looked 'more promising.'[38] 'My preference,' Vance wrote in his memoirs 'in dealing with human rights issues was to emphasize quiet diplomacy.'[39]

Brzezinski believed that 'quiet diplomacy' had its role. But that was too often a synonym for ignoring the issue entirely. Brzezinski then took measures to remove the radio services from the 'excessive political control' of the State Department. On March 22, 1977 President Carter, on Brzezinski's urging, requested an increase in funding that would double the operations of Radio Free Europe and Radio Liberty. The plan called for the construction of 16 new 250-kilowatt transmitters, five for the Voice of America and 11 for Radio Free Europe and Radio Liberty.[40] Brzezinski

---

32   P. Osnos, 'Carter Praised by Dissidents in Moscow,' *Washington Post*, March 1, 1977.

33   C. R. Whitney, 'Carter Rights Stand Worries Europe,' *New York Times*, March 5, 1977.

34   P. Osnos, 'Soviets Warn US Acts on Dissidents Cold Affect Ties,' *Washington Post*, February 21, 1977.

35   J. Hoagland, 'France Bars Comment on East Bloc Dissidents,' *Washington Post*, February 23, 1977.

36   M. Marder, 'Soviets Criticize US on SALT, Human Rights,' *Washington Post*, March 28, 1977.

37   S. Brown, *Faces of Power*, New York: Columbia University Press, 1983, p. 539.

38   D. Oberdorfer, 'Vance: Avoid Arrogance on Human Rights,' *Washington Post*, May 1, 1977.

39   C. Vance, *Hard Choices*, New York: Simon & Schuster 1983, p. 46.

40   See D. Binder, 'Carter Requests Funds for Big Increase in Broadcasts to Soviet Bloc,' *New York Times*, March 23, 1977.

also prepared a classified Presidential Directive that outlined the formal US policy toward Eastern Europe. The directive stated:

1. the US should cultivate a closer relationship with Eastern Europe for its own sake rather than as a by-product of détente with the Soviet Union;
2. the criteria for favorable treatment would be formulated in terms of their domestic policies as well as foreign policy independence from the USSR;
3. the administration should maintain regular contacts with representatives of the 'loyal opposition' in Eastern Europe: i.e. liberal intellectuals, artists and church leaders, as well as with government officials.[41]

Brzezinski's strategy of 'peaceful engagement' was having its greatest impact in Poland. The Polish leadership, burdened by a severe economic crisis and an emboldened opposition movement, was in a bind. The Carter Administration came into office with the clear signal that, henceforth, all financial assistance to Warsaw would be contingent on an adherence to the Helsinki Final Act. The day before Carter's inauguration the Polish government announced it was taking a 'softer line' on its opposition groups.[42]

Wojciech Jaruzelski, then the Polish Defense Minister, recalled Brzezinski's 'peaceful engagement' strategy was always seen as a severe threat to the Soviet control over Eastern Europe.

> The Polish government understood that Brzezinski's approach was very dangerous. Indeed, it was far more dangerous than that proposed by any other American politician or political scientist. But Brzezinski was also a Pole who never advocated radical changes that would lead to the shedding of blood. This was very important to him. He knew our history, our romanticism that we have in our blood and genes, and that bloody uprisings in the past had brought only regression. Of all the differences I had with Brzezinski, and there were many, I appreciated the fact that he, being convinced of the necessity of principal changes in Poland, still maintained it should be

41   See Z. Brzezinski, op. cit., pp. 296–7.

42   F. Lewis, 'Poland Softens Stand on Critics,' *New York Times*, January 20, 1977.

realized in an 'evolutionary' manner, avoiding situations that could lead to explosions.[43]

In May there occurred an incident that might have, in the past, led to violent upheavals. On May 7, 1977, Stanislaw Pyjas, a 19-year-old KOR member, was found beaten to death in Krakow. Few Poles believed the official explanation that Pyjas had fallen after a night of drinking. Pyjas' death became a galvanizing symbol in the struggle for human rights in Poland. Pyjas' memorial mass saw some 5,000 Poles marching silently through Krakow carrying candles and black flags. Polish Cardinal Karol Wojtyla, in a memorable homily, charged that Pyjas had 'fallen victim to the authorities' hatred of the democracy movement among the students.'[44]

The regime now faced a decision. There were some who argued that a crackdown was worth losing Western credits. Eleven members of KOR, including Adam Michnik, were jailed in the aftermath of Pyjas' funeral. On May 10, the day of Pyjas' funeral, President Carter and Brzezinski were in London attending the Western economic summit. West German Chancellor Helmut Schmidt, now a vocal critic of Carter's human rights policy, told Brzezinski that Radio Free Europe was a 'cold war relic' and 'contrary to détente,' and that he would like to 'get it out of Germany.'[45]

Brzezinski took a different point of view.

> I told him to just bear in mind that Radio Free Europe's presence in Munich is an integral part of the American military presence in Germany—and it's directly related to our sense of security in Europe. And you can't separate the two.[46]

Brzezinski insisted that keeping pressure on the Eastern European regimes would provide breathing room for the burgeoning opposition movements in the region. This was especially true as Soviet bloc regimes sought to burnish their image before the follow up conference to the Helsinki process was set to begin in Belgrade.

Brzezinski's strategy appeared to be bearing fruit in Poland. On July 22, in the midst of the preliminary Belgrade session, Gierek unexpectedly announced an

---

43   Interview Wojciech Jaruzelski, April 28, 2003, Warsaw, Poland.

44   P. Osnos, 'Current Unrest in Poland Reveals Rising Influence of Populace on Politics,' *Washington Post*, June 3, 1977.

45   Z. Brzezinski, op. cit., p. 293.

46   Interview with Z. Brezezinski, September 27, 2003, Washington, DC.

amnesty for a number of workers and members of KOR who had been imprisoned over the past year. Gierek, claimed one insider, did not want to be seen as a 'mobster' before the Belgrade Conference. He was also vitally concerned with maintaining Poland's liberal international reputation for the 'pragmatic purpose of preserving access to Western financial markets.'[47]

Gierek's act of clemency would dramatically impact on the future of the Polish opposition. Timothy Garton Ash noted that thereafter KOR activists were severely abused and harassed. But they retained enough freedom to solidify the links between KOR, the workers, and the Roman Catholic Church. A revolution had begun.[48]

The West European states remained skeptical. That same July, French President Giscard d'Estaing called an 'urgent meeting' with West German Chancellor Helmut Schmidt. The two leaders were seeking to curb President Carter's human rights campaign. In the joint press conference Giscard, who had recently entertained Soviet leader Leonid Brezhnev in Paris, argued Carter's human rights campaign had 'broken the code of conduct on détente' that prohibited interference in other nations internal affairs.[49]

As the year came to a close Brzezinski was attempting to covertly stoke the quiet revolution gathering momentum in Poland. Not everybody was convinced of the wisdom of this path. This was especially true in the State Department and certain sections of the CIA. Arnold Horelick, the National Intelligence Officer for the Soviet Union, wrote to the head of the CIA's analytical directorate, Robert Bowie, on November 18, 1977:

> This march of proposals was precipitated by Brzezinski's expression of interest last May on what more could be done via CIA against Soviet and East European targets. It is not clear to anyone in this building (CIA) what Zbig may have had in mind; I do not exclude the possibility that he had not thought that much about it before hand.

Three days later, on November 21, Horelick again wrote to Bowie expressing his concerns. 'In present circumstances, US policy interests in fostering greater

---

47   Lepak, p. 182. Some observers at the time were less enthusiastic about the long-term strategy of 'economic leverage.' See B. D. Nossiter, 'Threat to West Seen in Rising Soviet-Bloc Debt,' *Washington Post*, March 3, 1977.

48   Garton Ash, *The Polish Revolution. Solidarity*, London, Penguin Books, 1999, p. 21.

49   'Giscard, Schmidt on Détente,' *Washington Post*, July 19, 1977.

East European worker discontent, especially in Poland, are at least ambivalent (some would say that they are directly contradictory).'[50]

Brzezinski had indeed 'thought about it before hand.' Brzezinski advised President Carter to include Poland among the sites of his first major trip abroad as a means to 'encourage the processes of liberalization that were gathering momentum.'[51] He had also thought about how Carter's trip to Poland would differ sharply from the visit undertaken by Nixon and Kissinger on their way home from the 1972 Moscow summit.

Back then the Poles, seeking economic aid while engaging in a cultural crackdown, welcomed Nixon's form of détente. The highlight of Nixon's trip to Poland had been an economic discussion with Polish Prime Minister Piotr Jaroszewicz, an ideological hardliner, known as 'Moscow's man' in Warsaw.[52] As Nixon was toasting Jaroszewicz, Cardinal Stefan Wyszynski, the Polish Primate, was leading tens of thousands of Poles in a celebration of *Corpus Christi*. The new protocols of détente required that Nixon refrain from meeting with a religious leader out of favor with the government. And he did not.[53] Writing in the weeks after, Brzezinski bitterly referred to Nixon's visit to Poland as a tacit recognition of the Brezhnev Doctrine a 'legitimization' of the Soviet postwar gains in Eastern Europe.[54] Adam Michnik, among several Poles jailed in anticipation of the Nixon's visit, was deeply disturbed by the tenor of Nixon's visit. Michnik recalled:

> When Nixon came to Poland in 1972, members of the democratic oppo-
> sition were arrested. I wondered at that time whether it was because
> they were worried we would throw a bomb at him, or throw flowers at
> him. It was amazing. The Americans seemed to consider it a normal thing
> that people were imprisoned during this visit. They expressed abso-
> lutely no concern about it. Nixon did not offer any encouragement to
> the opposition. It was as if we were told 'resign yourself to your fate'.[55]

Brzezinski was determined that Carter's visit would be different. Yet the mere decision to send Carter to Poland met opposition from Vance and his special advisor for

---

50   R. M. Gates, *From the Shadows: The Ultimate Insider's Story of Five Presidents and How They Won the Cold War*, Simon & Schuster, 2007, p. 92.

51   Z. Brzezinski, op. cit., p. 297.

52   A. Korbonski, 'Soviet Policy Toward Poland,' in S. Meiklejohn Terry (ed.), *Soviet Policy in Eastern Europe*, New Haven, CT: Yale University Press, 1984, p. 66.

53   J. Feron, 'Nixon in Warsaw.' *New York Times*.

54   Z. Brzezinski, 'How the Cold War was Played,' *Foreign Affairs*, vol. 51, no. 1, October 1972, p. 201.

55   Interview with Adam Michnik, March 30, 2001, Warsaw, Poland.

Soviet Affairs, Marshall Shulman, who viewed it as too 'provocative' to the Soviet Union. Scholar Charles Gati recalled:

> Well, that was the climate. I can forgive those people who did not expect the weaknesses of the Soviet type systems were such that they could collapse. I didn't until very late. But not to expect that these regimes can moderate themselves and become more accommodating to their people and their citizens was inexcusable. The State Department was full of these people that took the view that we should take them as they are and make the best of it. I thought that was appeasement—and Brzezinski certainly had nothing to do with that.[56]

Air Force One touched down at Warsaw's Okecie airport on December 29, 1977. President Carter, shielding himself from the bitter December wind, was welcomed on the tarmac by Edward Gierek, who viewed the visit as a welcome distraction from deepening economic crisis and an emboldened opposition.

Carter, taking his cues from Brzezinski, visited the Tomb of the Unknown Solider and the monument honoring Poles who died in Warsaw in World War II. Carter then moved on to the Warsaw ghetto monument where he placed a wreath affixed with a yellow Star of David on the monument. He stood for ten seconds, head bowed, his left hand touching his forehead as if in prayer in respect for the thousands of Jews who held out in the walled ghetto against the Nazis during the uprising of 1943. Carter then proceeded to the Nike monument honoring the Polish resistance to the Nazi occupation. This move was particularly sensitive to Soviet officials, as it was a blatant reminder that Red Army troops remained poised across the Vistula during the 1944 uprising, as Warsaw—and the Polish Home Army—was obliterated by the Nazis.[57]

In the evening Carter stood before television cameras in a Warsaw hotel ballroom in the first ever press conference by an American President in Eastern Europe. Carter offered delicate praise to the relative moderation of Polish government. 'I think that our concept of human rights is preserved in Poland,' noted Carter, 'much better than other (Eastern) European nations with which I am familiar.' At the same time he offered his support to those struggling in the various opposition movements. Carter then announced that the US would provide Poland with $200

---

56   Interview with Charles Gati, September 13, 2001, Washington, DC.

57   J. T. Wooten, 'Carter in Warsaw on Start of Six-Nation Tour,' *New York Times*, December 30, 1977.

million in credits to buy food and feed grains—in addition to an earlier $300 million deal—to help make up for four years of Polish crop failures.[58]

This was the epitome of the carrot and stick, long inherent in Brzezinski's concept of 'peaceful engagement.' Timothy Garton Ash wrote,

> At a press conference, Carter loudly praised the Polish record on human rights and religious tolerance. In the next breath he announced a further $200 million of US credits. 'Linkage' could hardly be more explicit than that. If the KOR activists had still been imprisoned, it is doubtful if the credits would have flowed so freely.[59]

Brzezinski still had his biggest card to play. Brzezinski had hoped that Carter could meet privately with Cardinal Stefan Wyszynski, the 76-year-old Roman Catholic Primate of Poland. But the proposal gesture met with firm reaction from the State Department already wary of Carter's trip to Poland. Brzezinski then offered to meet with Wyszinski himself. This also met with opposition from the US ambassador in Warsaw.

Brzezinski then took matters into his own hands. Brzezinski, unbeknown to the State Department, simply arranged for him and the First Lady Rosalynn Carter to meet privately with the Cardinal. He was followed by the secret police, but they could do little to stop the semi-official mission. Brzezinski engaged in a 90-minute visit at the Cardinal's Warsaw residence, and delivered a letter from President Carter assuring the Cardinal, 'You have my prayers and respect; I share your faith, I admire what you represent. I seek the same goals.'[60]

On the last day of 1977 Carter ended his 35-hour stay in Poland. Adam Michnik, who was put in jail before Nixon's 1972 visit, discussed the difference of Carter's trip to Poland. Michnik argued:

> Carter's visit was completely different. Brzezinski, in a very clear way, referred to the Home Army tradition. Brzezinski met with Wyszynski, and this was the first signal that there was an 'other' Poland rather than Poland of Gierek and the Communists. On television Carter used the expression 'the countries under Soviet domination'—and it

---

58   Ibid.

59   T. Garton Ash, op. cit., p. 22. The fringes of the American right-wing seized on Brzezinski's trip to Poland to further their claim that he was in fact a closet communist.

60   D. A. Andelman, 'Brzezinski and Mrs. Carter Hold Discussions with Polish Cardinal,' *New York Times*, December 29, 1977.

was the first time that Poles had heard something like this. In short, it was a visit of hope.[61]

Bronislaw Geremek recalled a similar feeling:

> It was so important in the way in which it was organized. The Polish authorities tried to obtain from the Carter visit a sense of legitimacy. They did obtain it, paradoxically enough, with the Nixon visit, but not with the Carter visit. Why? Because Brzezinski from the beginning introduced, not meetings with the opposition, that would be impossible, but with the Church and the primate of Poland. Brzezinski's idea was that in order to have contact with the Polish society, real society, the Americans, and the President of the United States should have contact with the real representative of the Polish society, the Church. That changed the context in a very important way. Even before John Paul II came to the Vatican this visit gave a national and political dimension to the church—that was the beginning of a process—with the Pope's visit in 1979—that was the preparation of the appearance of the Solidarity movement.[62]

The Helsinki Final Act marked a turning point in the Cold War. Zbigniew Brzezinski was one of the few American voices who backed the idea of a broad multilateral conference to settle the outstanding issues of World War II. His primary motivation was to loosen the ossified divisions of Europe and allow the West to penetrate what was inaccurately assumed to be an 'Iron Curtain' separating the two blocs. But the Helsinki Final Act itself may have gone down in history as another Yalta had Brzezinski not rallied East European dissidents behind the broader meaning of 'Basket Three' and prodded a relatively inexperienced President Carter into making it the hallmark of his foreign policy toward the Soviet Union.

---

61   Interview with Adam Michnik, March 30, 2001, Warsaw, Poland.

62   Interview with Bronislaw Geremek, May 13, 2001, Warsaw, Poland.

Like many of his predecessors, Carter's administration was politically constrained with the Iran hostage situation, where 52 diplomats and citizens were held hostage for 444 days beginning on November 4, 1979. When President Carter attempted to bring back the hostages via an elite commando group, it ended in a logistical and human disaster because US helicopters were not used to the environmental challenges in Iran, mainly that of sandstorms. As a result, the botched rescue attempt to secure our citizens indicated that America had lost some of its military capabilities in a post-Vietnam era. This position of weakness, in part, caused President Carter to lose the 1980 election to Republican candidate Ronald Reagan.

Chapter 4: Identify the Following Key Players and Events

- Zbigniew Brzezinski
  - President Carter
- Soviets in Afghanistan
  - Boycott of the Olympics in Moscow
- Brzezinski and Kissinger strategies
  - Worldview of engagement
- Iran hostages

Discussion Questions

1. What were the differences in Zbigniew Brzezinski's and Henry Kissinger's views on the Soviet Union?
2. President Carter's worldview was that of engagement, human rights, and disarmament toward the Soviet Union. How did this worldview help his 1976 presidential campaign?
3. What is better foreign policy when dealing with the Soviet Union: to divide the world into spheres of influence and negotiate with governments, or to accept the ideological confrontation with the Soviet Union, that of human rights? Please explain.
4. What effect did President Carter's human rights campaign have on the Strategic Arms Limitation Talks (SALT)?
5. Brzezinski's directive outlining formal US policy toward Eastern Europe was a threat to the Soviet Union, especially in Poland. Please explain.

Comparative Essay

Directions: Read the following passage and write an essay that compares the actions of the United States during the Carter administration to that of President Barack Obama toward human rights in Russia.

The strength of focusing on human rights is that most people around the world believe in some form of human rights. The ideology of fighting for the rights of others has profoundly changed the way in which America engages in foreign policy. Search the Internet for articles about human rights concerning the Soviet Union under the Carter administration, then look for similar articles concerning Russia under the Obama administration. Which groups of people are being suppressed? Compare President Obama's administration to that of President Carter concerning human rights. What are the results from the Carter presidency and that of President Obama? Was it worth fighting for human rights? Was the Soviet Union or Russia weakened by this US policy?

Time Line

- 1977 January—President Carter takes office
- 1979 June—Soviet leader Brezhnev and President Carter sign SALT II
- 1979 December—Soviets invade Afghanistan
- 1980 February—President Carter demands that the Soviets withdraw from Afghanistan
- 1980 March—President Carter declares a boycott on the Summer Olympic Games in Moscow

Chapter 5

The Reagan Revolution, 1981

Chapter Focus

How was Ronald Reagan the man influenced by Communism? Can you give any specific examples? How did Ronald Reagan view the progressive tax system as an influence toward Communism? Can you give any specific examples? How did Ronald Reagan characterize "good versus evil?" Can you give any specific examples?

The October 28, 1980, presidential debate between President Jimmy Carter and Governor Ronald Reagan sparked new interest in American politics. The outsider Jimmy Carter versus the ultimate outsider Ronald Reagan. Both men capable debaters, both men informed citizens, both men with experience in government—the two best choices for America. Journalist Marvin Stone, editor of *U.S. News and World Report*, asked Governor Reagan the first question:

> *"... President Carter's been criticized for responding late to aggressive Soviet impulses, for insufficient buildup of our Armed Forces, and a paralysis in dealing with Afghanistan and Iran. You have been criticized for being all too quick to advocate the use of lots of muscle, military action, to deal with foreign crises. Specifically, what are the differences between the two of you on the uses of American military power?"*

"GOVERNOR REAGAN. I don't know what the differences might be, because I don't know what Mr. Carter's policies are. I do know what he has said about mine. And I'm only here to tell you that I believe with all my heart that our first priority must be world peace, and that use of force is always and only a last resort, when everything else has failed, and then only with regard to our national security.

Now, I believe, also that this meeting, this mission, this responsibility for preserving the peace, which I believe is a responsibility peculiar to our country, that we cannot shirk our responsibility as the leader of the Free World, because we're the only one that can do it. And therefore, the burden of maintaining the peace falls on us. And to maintain that peace requires strength. America has never gotten in a war because we were too strong. We can get into a war by letting events get out of hand, as they have in the last three years under the foreign policies of this administration of Mr. Carter's, until we're faced each time with a crisis. And good management in preserving the peace requires that we control the events and try to intercept before they become a crisis.

But I have seen four wars in my lifetime. I'm a father of sons; I have a grandson. I don't ever want to see another generation of young Americans bleed their lives into sandy beachheads in the Pacific, or rice paddies and jungles in Asia, or the muddy, bloody battlefields of Europe."[1]

The sincerity, honesty, and raw emotion from Governor Ronald Reagan captivated the audience. Reagan set the tone for the entire evening. Although President Jimmy Carter's answers to the panel of journalists were equally as compelling and honest, the American people were ready for a new start. A new decade was emerging, with new ways of thinking, new science and technologies. Although America was still in a Cold War with the Soviets, for some reason it seemed different in 1980, as if the world was supposed to change, as if the wind had changed and Reagan was the new captain keeping Americans on course. In fact, staying on course seemed to be preferred at this time by many American voters. There was something different about

---

1   http://www.presidency.ucsb.edu/ws/index.php?pid=29408 (*Presidential Debate in Cleveland, 1980*)

Ronald Reagan. He possessed a charisma that people admired and were drawn to, which was very evident on election night, when he won 489 electoral votes to Carter's 49 electoral votes, also winning the popular vote by approximately 43 to 35 million.[2]

To fully understand Ronald Reagan and his perception of the Cold War, one has to experience his previous life before he became president of the United States.

Read the following article by Robert C. Rowland and John M. Jones entitled *Ronald Reagan and the Evolution of Cold War Rhetoric and Policies.*

---

2   https://www.britannica.com/event/United-States-presidential-election-of-1980

Ronald Reagan and the Evolution of Cold War Rhetoric and Policies

Robert C. Rowland and John M. Jones

R onald Reagan's address to the British Parliament can be understood only when situated within the larger context of the cold war and Reagan's rhetorical response to it. In this chapter we trace U.S. policy in the cold war through three periods: genesis, stasis, and détente. It is not our intention to provide a detailed history of the cold war but rather to lay out a brief historical background drawing upon widely recognized sources. We also trace the development of the anticommunist rhetoric of Ronald Reagan. Finally, we discuss the events and rhetoric from the first eighteen months of the Reagan presidency, which set the stage for the Westminster address.

Genesis of the Cold War, 1945–1949

U.S. cold war policy in the late 1940s was one of containment, the genesis of which came from an eight-thousand-word telegram from George Kennan, a U.S. Foreign Service officer serving in Moscow in 1946. In what became known as the "Long Telegram," Kennan told the State Department that "Soviet hostility toward the capitalist world was inevitable and immutable because it provided the justification for the oppressive totalitarian system the communists had imposed upon the Soviet people."[1] He opposed any efforts to accommodate the Soviet Union and insisted that the proper U.S. policy for the time was a "long-term, patient but firm and

---

1   Quoted in Ronald E. Powaski, *The Cold War: The United States and the Soviet Union, 1917–1991,* 70. Kennan favored a policy that curbed the expansion of the Soviet Union until "a more moderate form of government came into being in the Soviet Union." Ibid.

Robert C. Rowland and John M. Jones, "Ronald Reagan and the Evolution of Cold War Rhetoric and Policies," *Reagan at Westminster: Foreshadowing the End of the Cold War*, pp. 20-36, 130-133. Copyright © 2010 by Texas A&M University Press. Reprinted with permission.

vigilant containment of communism."[2] This telegram set the stage for President Harry Truman's cold war policy and the actions that followed.

The first major action took place in 1947, when the British, facing an economic crisis, were no longer able to provide aid to Greece, which was in the midst of a civil war involving communist insurgents. In response, Truman persuaded Congress to approve $300 million in aid for Greece and $100 million for Turkey, taking "the first step in a global ideological crusade against communism."[3] This action marked the birth of the Truman Doctrine, committing the United States to "support free peoples who are resisting attempted subjugation by armed minorities or by outside pressures" and assisting these nations as they endeavored to "work out their own destinies in their own way."[4] Elizabeth Edwards Spalding has called the doctrine "the primary building block of containment and postwar liberal internationalism."[5] According to historian Howard Jones, the Truman Doctrine "signaled the administration's willingness to engage the struggle against communism on all fronts—social, political, and economic as well as military."[6] Out of this policy came such actions as the Berlin Airlift, the creation of NATO, military involvement in Korea, and a massive effort to rebuild Western Europe.

In June 1947, Secretary of State George C. Marshall unveiled the European Recovery Program, dedicating the United States "to nothing less than the reconstruction of Europe."[7] Marshall was concerned that conditions of "hunger, poverty, and despair" would likely "cause Europeans to vote their own communists into office, who then would obediently serve Moscow's wishes."[8] To prevent this from occurring, the United States over the next five years spent more than $12 billion to rebuild Europe. The plan "help[ed] to ensure that Western Europe remained politically stable, sufficiently conservative to protect

---

2   John Lewis Gaddis, *The Cold War: A New History*, 29.

3   Powaski, *Cold War*, 72.

4   Harry S. Truman, "The Truman Doctrine," March 12, 1947, http://www.americanrhetoric .com/speeches/harrystrumantrumandoctrine.html, 4.

5   Elizabeth Edwards Spalding, *The First Cold Warrior: Harry Truman, Containment, and the Remaking of Liberal Internationalism*, 71.

6   Howard Jones, *A New Kind of War: America's Global Strategy and the Truman Doctrine in Greece*, 36.

7   Gaddis, *Cold War*, 31.

8   Ibid., 32.

America's European economic investments, and, as a result less susceptible to Soviet pressure."[9]

Stasis, 1950–1963

In the early 1950s containment remained the primary cold war policy of the United States. In June 1950 the Korean War began as Kim Il-sung launched an invasion of South Korea, having received the support of Joseph Stalin. Because the invasion had been so "blatant" and "appeared to challenge the entire structure of postwar collective security," Truman very quickly made the decision to send troops.[10] The conflict lasted until July 1953, a few months after Stalin's death.

By that time, a new president, Dwight Eisenhower, had been elected. Eisenhower was determined to avoid "Korea-like limited wars" in the future, believing that such conflicts allowed the communists to have control over when and where the United States would deploy its forces.[11] In 1954 Eisenhower and his secretary of state, John Foster Dulles, unveiled a new policy for dealing with the Soviets. The United States would "react massively, with nuclear weapons, in the event of communist aggression at any level, strategic or tactical."[12] Eisenhower and Dulles believed that the threat of a massive nuclear retaliation would ensure that "no war at all would take place."[13] Nuclear forces also were less expensive than conventional ones. Accordingly, during Eisenhower's presidency the air force was expanded while the army and navy were reduced in size. This "New Look" for the military also included increased production of ballistic missiles.[14]

Eisenhower also was willing to use covert action. He used the CIA to overthrow the Iranian government in 1953 and to depose the Guatemalan president in 1954. As Ronald Powaski observes, "Covert operations in the Third World mushroomed during his tenure."[15] But the primary focus of the 1950s was a shift from reliance

---

9 Powaski, *Cold War,* 73.

10 Gaddis, *Cold War,* 43.

11 Ibid., 64.

12 Powaski, *Cold War,* 102.

13 Gaddis, *Cold War,* 68. Ned O'Gorman argues that Eisenhower "assumed a priestly mantle, performing the American synecdochal sublime through a rhetoric of national absolution, spiritual reinterpretation, and calls for human transformation." Ned O'Gorman, "Eisenhower and the American Sublime," 47.

14 Powaski, *Cold War,* 102.

15 Ibid., 133.

on conventional forces to a focus on nuclear armaments. By 1960, the nuclear arms race between the United States and the Soviet Union clearly was under way.

After the 1960 election, President John F. Kennedy was astonished to learn that "the only war plan Eisenhower had left behind would have required the *simultaneous* use of well over 3,000 nuclear weapons against *all* communist countries." In response, Kennedy charged Defense Secretary Robert McNamara with expanding the options for fighting a nuclear war and also sought to "get the Soviets to agree on what the rules for such combat might be."[16] McNamara concluded that "each side should target the other's cities, with a view to causing the maximum number of casualties possible," a strategy known as mutually assured destruction or MAD.[17] As John Lewis Gaddis observes, "What kept war from breaking out in the fall of 1962 [the Cuban missile crisis] was the irrationality, on both sides, of sheer terror. That is what Churchill had foreseen when he saw hope in an 'equality of annihilation.' It is what Eisenhower had understood when he ruled out fighting limited nuclear wars."[18] What Churchill and Eisenhower had understood was simply "that the advent of nuclear weapons meant that war could no longer be an instrument of statecraft—rather the survival of the states required that there be no war at all."[19] This policy essentially remained in place until the 1980s.

In addition to instituting the MAD policy, the Kennedy administration became the first to engage in serious negotiation to produce nuclear arms control agreements. In 1963, the Limited Test Ban Treaty was signed, with the United States and the Soviet Union both agreeing not to test nuclear weapons in the atmosphere.[20] This treaty was the first in a series of agreements that would be signed by the two nations in the years that followed. Like the policy of mutually assured destruction, the pursuit of arms limitation agreements became a focus of U.S. foreign policy.

Containment also continued to be an integral part of U.S. policy during these years. Kennedy increased the number of military advisors in South Vietnam from 700 to 16,700. He allowed the advisors to participate in combat and also approved a coup led by the CIA that overthrew South Vietnam's president, Ngo Dinh Diem. After the Kennedy assassination, President Lyndon Johnson inherited the U.S.

---

16   Gaddis, *Cold War,* 79.

17   Ibid., 80.

18   Ibid.

19   Ibid., 80–81.

20   Michael R. Beschloss, *The Crisis Years: Kennedy and Khrushchev, 1960–1963,* 599.

commitment to South Vietnam and "transformed Kennedy's program of limited U.S. assistance into an open-ended commitment to defend that country."[21]

The period between 1950 and 1963 saw not only a commitment to containing communism but also a shift from a strategy based largely on conventional forces to one that included the possible use of nuclear weapons. During these years, the seeds of détente were sown.

Détente, 1964–1980

In 1964 containment was still a dominant part of American foreign policy, but over the next four years containment would "experience its first significant failures in the Third World."[22] Even the massive commitment of troops to Southeast Asia could not hold off the communist insurgency, and the United States found itself in a no-win situation. Ironically, it was during a time of war that serious efforts at détente with the Soviet Union began.

Concerned about the increase in Soviet nuclear weaponry and hoping warmer relations would prompt the Soviets to help bring North Vietnam to the negotiating table, President Johnson began to pursue improved relations.[23] This effort culminated in the signing of the Nuclear Nonproliferation Treaty in 1968, which opened the door for future discussion with the Soviets. Johnson also pushed for an antiballistic missile ban at a time when a program to create a missile defense system was under way, and he made an effort to begin Strategic Arms Limitation Talks (SALT). Although he left office without accomplishing these objectives, his successor would continue to move toward détente.

Several factors motivated President Richard Nixon to continue what his predecessor had begun. He also hoped that détente with the Soviets would motivate North Vietnam to negotiate peace. Nixon also sought the swift conclusion of a SALT agreement to cap the growth of Soviet nuclear weaponry, which by that time was roughly equal to that of the United States.[24] Furthermore, Nixon hoped that détente might "blunt Soviet interest in attempting to confront the United States and its core allies" and "minimize confrontation in marginal areas and provide,

---

21   Powaski, *Cold War,* 155.

22   Ibid., 166.

23   Ibid., 163.

24   Ibid., 167.

at least, alternative possibilities in the major ones."[25] Nixon's efforts at détente were not limited to the Soviet Union, and he made a groundbreaking trip to China in February 1972. This trip was followed by a summit meeting with Soviet leader Leonid Brezhnev in May 1972. At the latter meeting, Nixon and Brezhnev signed the Anti-Ballistic Missile Treaty and the Interim Agreement. It would prove to be détente's finest hour and one of the most significant accomplishments of the Nixon presidency.

After Nixon resigned in 1974, President Gerald Ford kept Nixon's secretary of state, Henry Kissinger, and continued to pursue détente. When Ronald Reagan challenged Ford for the Republican presidential nomination in 1976, détente became one of the most salient issues of the campaign. Under attack from Reagan, Ford stopped using the word *détente,* but the policy remained in place.

From 1977 through 1979, Jimmy Carter continued to support détente, though, as Raymond Garthoff reports, his policy was really "an erratic mix, predominantly détente in 1977 and predominantly competitive coexistence in 1978 and 1979."[26] By that time, détente was in decline. Efforts at negotiating a SALT II treaty had proven unsuccessful. Furthermore, the Soviet Union had shown aggressive tendencies by invading Afghanistan in December 1979. In response, Carter imposed a grain embargo against the Soviet Union and announced that the United States would not send a team to the 1980 Summer Olympics in Moscow. He also increased defense spending, and the United States began to assist anti-Soviet fighters in Afghanistan. By 1980 Carter's policy was "a sharp move to containment, although with the avowed aim of returning to détente if Soviet behavior permitted it."[27] The decline of détente, increased Soviet aggression, and the beginning of a military buildup by the Carter administration set the stage for Reagan's approach to the Soviet Union.

Development of Reagan's Rhetoric

The 1940s were transformational years for Ronald Reagan. Through personal experiences in Hollywood, he became convinced that the threat of communism should be taken as seriously as fascism.[28] As biographer Paul Kengor points out,

---

25   Raymond L. Garthoff, *Détente and Confrontation: American-Soviet Relations from Nixon to Reagan,* 29.

26   Ibid., 39.

27   Ibid.

28   Ronald Reagan, *An American Life,* 106.

"It was during this time that he was hammered into an iron-clad anti-communist."[29] The transformation began shortly after the end of World War II. Reagan strongly suspected that communists maintained a presence in Hollywood, a view now supported by some, but not all, observers.[30] The actor became convinced of communist influence in the industry during the Conference of Studio Unions (CSU) strike, which began in September 1946. According to Reagan, the walkout, which ostensibly was for the purpose of improving wages and working conditions, was an attempt to help CSU leader Herb Sorrell gain jurisdictional control "over a group of workers within the IATSE [International Association of Theatrical and Stage Employees] called Set Erectors."[31] Reagan, along with other actors, fought successfully against this effort, and the strike ended in the spring of 1947.[32]

During the strike, Reagan was approached by the FBI and asked to become an informant. He agreed to do so and met with agents from time to time to "discuss things that were going on in Hollywood."[33] At the same time, the House Un-American Activities Committee (HUAC) began its investigations with the goal of declaring the Communist Party illegal.[34] On October 25, 1947, Reagan appeared before the committee. His testimony contained three rhetorical patterns—a strong denunciation of communism, his story of the battle against communists in Hollywood, and Reagan's personal conviction that democracy was strong enough to stand on its own.

As he answered questions, Reagan made clear his disdain for communism, saying, "I detest, I abhor their philosophy, but I detest more than that their tactics, which are those of the fifth column and are dishonest."[35] He also recalled the battle against communists in Hollywood and testified that the industry as a whole had "exposed their lies" and "prevented them from, with their usual tactics, trying to run a majority of an organization with a well organized minority."[36]

Evident as his opposition to communism was, however, it was equally clear that Reagan did not believe that the party should be outlawed: "So that fundamentally

29   Paul Kengor, *The Crusader: Ronald Reagan and the Fall of Communism,* 12.

30   For example, Lou Cannon reports that communists "enjoyed two periods of influence in Hollywood": in the late 1930s and again in the mid-1940s. See L. Cannon, *President Reagan,* 73–74.

31   Reagan, *An American Life,* 107.

32   L. Cannon, *President Reagan,* 76.

33   Reagan, *An American Life,* 111.

34   Anne Edwards, *Early Reagan: The Rise to Power,* 338.

35   Ibid., 349.

36   Ibid., 346–47.

I would say that in opposing those people that the best thing to do is to make democracy work. In the Screen Actors Guild we made it work by insuring [sic] everyone a vote and by keeping everyone informed. I believe that as Thomas Jefferson put it, if all the American people know all of the facts they will never make a mistake."[37] Reagan believed that the most important weapon in the battle against communism was democracy itself, which, if allowed to flourish, would make outlawing the Communist Party unnecessary. He told the committee, "We have spent 170 years in this country on the basis that democracy is strong enough to stand up and fight against the inroads of any ideology." For that reason, he opposed the idea of outlawing "any political party on the basis of its ideology."[38]

Although Reagan's HUAC testimony itself was, for the time, quite moderate, Reagan's actions and words in the late 1940s have been sharply criticized. Some have argued strongly that his claim of a communist threat to Hollywood was grossly exaggerated. Moreover, becoming an informant for the FBI and associating himself with the House Un-American Activities Committee, which gave rise to "witch hunts" and destroyed the careers of hundreds of artists, created no small amount of controversy. It is understandable why liberals both then and in the early 1980s were critical of his actions.[39]

Whether one supports or opposes Reagan's actions in the 1940s, this much is clear: Reagan rhetorically defined the cold war as an ideological battle and opposed any effort to suppress free expression in the marketplace of ideas. Years later at Westminster, he echoed the theme that democracy inevitably would prevail in an ideological struggle with communism.

The 1950s and early 1960s witnessed a hardening of Reagan's anticommunist discourse. His rhetoric in this period can be defined by three themes: the moral battle between good and evil, the concept of "encroaching control," and his belief that the United States could win the cold war. During this period, Reagan made some of his most extreme statements about communism and the cold war. While his opposition to communism would not waver as the years passed, he eventually

---

37 Ibid., 348.

38 Ibid.

39 Michael Schaller suggested that the influence of communists in Hollywood was only "minuscule" and that "when asked to cite examples of Red influence [studio executives] did little more than point to scripts that showed Indians or African-Americans in sympathetic scenes." Michael Schaller, *Reckoning with Reagan: America and Its President in the 1980s*, 9. Biographer Lou Cannon, while acknowledging some communist influence in Hollywood, also contends that Reagan later "exaggerate[d] the danger the communists had posed to the film industry, quoting approvingly from the findings of the committee and denying that a blacklist really existed." See L. Cannon, *President Reagan*, 84.

dropped the most inflammatory elements of his rhetoric as he began appealing to a broader audience beyond the conservative movement.

But for the time being, Reagan clearly saw the struggle against communism as an ongoing fight between good and evil. In Reagan's estimation, those who championed freedom were inherently good while freedom's opponents were evil. America, he proclaimed, was the epitome of good and had been divinely set apart to be the "last best hope of man on earth."[40] In a commencement address delivered at William Woods College while American and NATO forces were defending the 38th parallel in Korea, Reagan defined the nature of the struggle: "It's the same old battle. We met it under the name of Hitlerism; we met it under the name of Kaiserism; and we've met it back through the ages in the name of every conqueror that has ever set upon a course of establishing his rule over mankind."[41]

The struggle against communism was to Reagan a perpetual battle between light and darkness, right and wrong, freedom and bondage. Five years later, at Eureka College, Reagan echoed these sentiments, calling the cold war "the oldest struggle of humankind, as old as man himself," a conflict "between those who believe in the sanctity of the individual and those who believe in the supremacy of the state."[42] The Soviet Union was an "evil force" and "the best organized and the most capable enemy of freedom and of right and decency that has ever been."[43] That worldview would later be a prominent feature of his presidential rhetoric. Reagan clearly saw the struggle in moral terms, and in that sense his discourse was consistent with the Truman Doctrine. He also believed that America was a light for the world that could "push back the darkness" of communism.[44]

In Reagan's view, America could either "push back the darkness" or slowly become engulfed by it. His concern that America gradually could drift toward communism was the basis for the second theme, that of encroaching control. As he toured the United States in the late 1950s and early 1960s, speaking at General Electric plants, he warned that the nation was in danger of drifting toward socialism and unwittingly falling into the hands of the communists. Using a slippery slope argument, Reagan contended that each new government program or regulation

---

40   Ronald Reagan, "Commencement Address at William Woods College," May 3, 1952, 13, Pre-Presidential Speech Files, Ronald Reagan Presidential Library (hereafter, Speech Files, RRPL).

41   Ibid., 9.

42   Ronald Reagan, "Commencement Address at Eureka College," June 7, 1957, in Ritter and Henry, *Ronald Reagan,* 129.

43   Ibid., 130.

44   Reagan, "Address at William Woods College," 13.

resulted in a loss of individual freedom. Thus, he urged the ordinary citizen to "analyze very carefully to see whether the suggested service is worth the personal freedom which you must forgo in return."[45] Reagan was convinced that if the federal government grew unchecked, individual freedom would erode incrementally, one government program at a time, until all of our freedoms had disappeared. He called this process "encroaching control," arguing that the Soviets could use it to destroy American democracy: "They are convinced that we will abandon our democratic institutions one by one under the stress of constant pressure. Nikita Khrushchev said, 'We cannot expect the Americans to jump from capitalism to communism. However, we can assist their leaders in giving Americans small doses of socialism until they suddenly awake to find they have communism.'"[46]

The small doses of socialism, in Reagan's view, included the progressive tax system, excessive federal regulations, mandatory payment into the Social Security system, and a host of other government programs. Reagan's rhetoric from this period is significant in part because it linked the three most fundamental tenets of his ideology: limiting the size and power of the federal government, reducing the tax burden, and staunch opposition to communism. Taxes and government, he argued, must be restrained to prevent the United States from traveling down a gradual but very slippery slope that ultimately would lead to communism.

It was not enough, however, to *not lose* the ideological struggle. Reagan believed that the cold war was winnable and that the United States, by embracing a doctrine of peace through strength, could prevail. Peace through strength thus became the third overarching theme of this period. To Reagan, the stakes were high. "In another decade," he told one audience, "the world will be headed either in the direction of freedom or slavery." He termed peaceful coexistence "a satanic, diabolical device of the enemy" and warned that "we must save [freedom] now or spend our sunset years telling our children and our children's children what it was like when men were free."[47] Reagan also castigated those who believed that "if they can take us a little to the left … that Russia will give up some of her brutality [and] the lion and the lamb will lie down together."[48] He blatantly condemned what he called "a policy of accommodation with the Soviet Union."[49] He dismissed

---

45   Reagan, "Address at Eureka College," 133.

46   Ronald Reagan, "Encroaching Control," May 8, 1961, 4, Speech Files, RRPL.

47   Ibid., 3.

48   Ronald Reagan, "Address to Employees of Forest Lawn," November 2, 1961, 3, Speech Files, RRPL.

49   Ronald Reagan, "Are Liberals Really Liberal?" ca. 1963, in *Reagan, In His Own Hand: The Writings of Ronald Reagan That Reveal His Revolutionary Vision for America,* 439.

such a view as "based on pure conjecture that maybe communism will mellow and recognize that our way is better." Following such a course, Reagan argued, would bring about the day when "[the Soviet Union] will be stronger, thanks to us and then perhaps we will see how close accommodation and appeasement are."[50]

Rather than a policy of accommodation, Reagan suggested that the Soviets were "more likely to recognize [that our way of life is better] and modify their stand if we let their economy come unhinged so that the contrast is apparent." Reagan believed that the Soviet economy was weak and should be allowed to grow weaker until it disintegrated. In his words, "We can make those rockets into bridge lamps by being so strong the enemy has no choice [but to negotiate]."[51] The result would be victory for the free world and peaceful coexistence with an enemy who had seen the error of its ways.

From 1950 to 1963, Reagan's rhetoric emphasized the struggle of good versus evil, the danger of encroaching control, and the possibility of an American victory in the cold war. In Reagan's judgment, the key to victory lay in the fundamental flaws of the Soviet system. It was clear to him that if accommodation were eschewed in favor of a strategy that put a strain on the Soviet economy, the entire Soviet system could change and the cold war could end. He also hinted at what became the core idea of the Westminster address: the power of liberal democratic ideals.

Reagan's rhetoric between 1964 and 1980 contained five overarching themes: a moral battle of good versus evil, rejection of accommodation, the doctrine of peace through strength, opposition to détente, and a commitment to the dual objectives of preserving the peace and winning the cold war. His discourse during this period began on a confrontational note, continuing themes in his rhetoric from the time of stasis. Over time, however, the danger of nuclear war and the necessity of peace became a more significant part of Reagan's rhetoric.

As in the previous period, Reagan argued that the enemy in Moscow was trying to impose upon the world "its belief that the end justifies the means, that there is no morality except that which furthers the cause we are trying to put over."[52] In Reagan's words, the enemy possessed "a missionary zeal to bless the world with their

---

50   Ibid., 442.

51   Ibid.

52   Ronald Reagan, "Transcript of Remarks on the *Joey Bishop Show*," June 5, 1968, 2.

ideology whether the world wants it or not."[53] Once again Reagan had phrased the struggle against communism in moral terms.

Because the enemy was evil and the struggle was moral in nature, Reagan strongly rejected the doctrine of accommodation. In a televised address supporting Barry Goldwater's campaign for president, he denounced what he called "a utopian solution of peace without victory," warning that "every lesson of history tells us that the greater risk lies in appeasement." Such a strategy, he believed, "gives us no choice between peace and war, only between fight and surrender."[54] Continuing to accommodate, Reagan suggested, eventually would bring about surrender on the part of the United States because "by that time we will have been weakened from within spiritually, morally, and economically." Yet Reagan was confident that the American people understood the importance of saying to the enemy, "There is a price we will not pay." America, in Reagan's judgment, must choose to "preserve this last best hope of man on earth" rather than "sentencing them to take the last step into a thousand years of darkness."[55] He had every confidence that the American people would choose preservation of hope over the darkness.

Rather than attempting to accommodate (or, in his view, appease) the Soviets, Reagan preferred a policy of peace through strength. Between 1964 and 1980, Reagan placed tremendous emphasis on being militarily stronger than the Soviets. In 1967, he told the Young Republicans group, "We can—we must—we will co-exist with the communists, but only when we can deal through a position of strength."[56] In another address, he expressed a concern that the United States might be falling behind the Soviet Union in nuclear arms. "If we want to continue living in the free world," he said, "we must have a military capability second to none."[57]

Living in a free world would not be possible, he believed, if the United States did not take a strong stand against Moscow. For that reason, Reagan strongly denounced détente. To him it was not a step toward peace or "an assurance against that horror of horrors—nuclear war." Instead, it was a policy that would benefit the Soviets more than the United States. Détente, he said, led to "increased communist influence in Italy, France, and Great Britain, increases in the Soviet

53   Ronald Reagan, "Remarks at the 60th Meeting of the Chamber of Commerce of the United States," May 1, 1972, 2, Speech Files, RRPL.

54   Ronald Reagan, "A Time for Choosing," October 27, 1964, 35.

55   Ibid., 36.

56   Ronald Reagan, "Remarks at Young Republicans' Convention," Omaha, Nebr., June 22, 1963, 7, Speech Files, RRPL.

57   Ronald Reagan, "Excerpt from Remarks by Governor Reagan," March 30, 1974, 3.

naval strength, the terrorist activities we have been unable to halt, and the Soviet Union's arrogant violations of the SALT agreements." It was, in his view, a policy in which "they arm and we limit."[58] Reagan favored a policy in which the United States increased its military might to surpass that of the Soviet Union. This issue would be one of the most important during the presidential primary campaign in which Reagan challenged Gerald Ford for the Republican nomination in 1976. He criticized the sitting president for pursuing what he called "the one-way street of détente" and for allowing the United States to fall behind the Soviet Union in nuclear capabilities.[59]

This belief in the need for military strength, however, should not be understood to mean that Reagan did not desire peace. As we make clear in chapter 5, avoiding a nuclear war was of paramount importance to him. Nowhere was this goal clearer than in his remarks at the close of the 1976 Republican National Convention, when he spoke of the arms race and the dangers of nuclear war, saying, "We live in a world in which the great powers have poised and aimed at each other horrible missiles of destruction, nuclear weapons that can in a matter of minutes arrive at each other's country and destroy, virtually the entire civilized world." He then expressed the hope that in one hundred years people would say, "Thank God for those people in 1976 who headed off that loss of freedom, who kept us now one hundred years later free, who kept our world from nuclear destruction."[60] This brief address revealed Reagan's commitment not only to protect American freedom from its enemies but also to avert a nuclear disaster.

During the 1980 election campaign, many Americans feared that a Reagan presidency would increase the risk of war with the Soviet Union. In one Gallup poll, 46 percent thought Jimmy Carter was "most likely to keep the country out of a war," while only 31 percent believed that Ronald Reagan was most likely to accomplish this aim.[61] Therefore, in order to defeat President Carter, Reagan had to reassure the American people of his commitment to peace. To accomplish this objective, Reagan made peace, along with neighborhood, work, freedom, and family primary themes of his campaign rhetoric. One example of Reagan expressing a commitment to peace was during a televised speech delivered just fifteen days before the election, in which he spoke "not as a candidate for the

---

58   Ronald Reagan, "Détente," Copley News Service, November 10, 1975, 2.

59   Ronald Reagan, "Remarks by Ronald Reagan," March 9, 1976, 1, stump speech delivered in several sites in Illinois, Speech Files, RRPL.

60   Ronald Reagan, "Remarks at the 31st Republican National Convention," August 19, 1976, 2.

61   Cited in Kiron Skinner et al., "The Strategy of Campaigning," 99.

presidency, but as a citizen, a parent—in fact, a grandparent—who shares with you the deep and abiding hope for peace."[62] He outlined nine steps for peace, three of which were the "restoration of a margin of safety in defense planning," an effort to "strengthen the quality of our armed services," and "a realistic strategic arms reduction policy."[63] Although Reagan clearly favored a military buildup, he argued that such a move was a means to eventually "sit down with the Soviet Union for as long as it takes to negotiate a balanced and equitable arms limitation agreement, designed to improve the prospects for peace."[64] Reagan continued to position himself as the candidate of peace throughout the campaign. Many suspected (or feared) that Reagan's commitment to peace was more rhetorical than actual. Despite these doubts, the rhetorical effort clearly succeeded at reassuring the American people, and on November 4, 1980, Reagan defeated Carter in a landslide and soon would become directly responsible for U.S. policy toward the Soviet Union.

Reagan's Soviet rhetoric from the 1940s through the 1980 campaign was defined by both continuity and evolution. Reagan's distaste for communism and all forms of totalitarianism, along with his support for liberal democracy, and a view that a strong defense policy was the best approach to the Soviets are themes evident in his rhetoric throughout the period. At the same time, as he became a public figure, his rhetoric became less strident and the importance of avoiding war and keeping the peace became more prominent themes. It was not so much that Reagan's message changed dramatically as the relationship among the themes became clearer; his argument became more nuanced, and his language softened. This evolution would be reflected in the address at Westminster.

Early Days in the Reagan Presidency

Reagan came into office with little in the way of foreign policy experience. Moreover, he was not a master of policy detail, preferring to speak in broad themes and leave the specifics to his subordinates. What he brought to Washington, however,

---

62   Ronald Reagan, "A Strategy of Peace for the 80s," 1.

63   Ibid., 3.

64   Ibid., 5.

was a commitment to policies and rhetoric that were a departure from détente and containment.

First, President Reagan was committed to building up American defense capabilities. His administration brought about the largest peacetime military buildup in U.S. history. This expansion included thousands of new aircraft, construction of the B-1 bomber, the Stealth bomber, and Trident submarines, and a massive increase in navy ships, as well as a continuation of the MX missile program.[65] John Lewis Gaddis reports that "by 1985 the Pentagon's budget was almost twice what it had been in 1980."[66] The buildup met with opposition from critics inside and outside the administration. On the outside, many feared that the buildup would cause the arms race to escalate, bringing the nation closer to war. Inside, some believed that the buildup would cause increased budget deficits, thus harming the nation's economy.[67] Despite the opposition, Reagan insisted on the expansion.

Second, Reagan shifted American foreign policy from a defensive to an offensive posture, but it was an offensive posture that rejected war or any policy that risked war. For years, the focus of American defense policy had been on either containment, a policy that endeavored simply to keep communism from spreading any further, or détente, whereby the United States pursued warmer relations with the Soviets. Reagan was unique among major figures in that since the early 1960s he had maintained that the cold war need not remain a stalemate. Instead, he had argued that the United States could prevail in the conflict, and he brought that belief to the White House, summarizing his cold war policy in a single sentence—"We win, they lose."[68] Sensing a weak adversary, Reagan clearly believed that the time was right to go on the offensive. Yet as Kiron Skinner and others have argued, Reagan was focused on "how to defeat the Soviets *peacefully.*"[69]

Finally, Reagan launched a rhetorical attack on the Soviet Union that in some ways resembled his cold war rhetoric of the 1950s and 1960s. In his judgment, the struggle remained a moral one and the Soviet leadership was still evil. Thus, in an early press conference, the new president accused the Soviets of being willing "to commit any crime, to lie, to cheat" in order to accomplish their

---

65   Dinesh D'Souza, *Ronald Reagan: How an Ordinary Man Became an Extraordinary Leader,* 143.

66   Gaddis, *Cold War,* 225.

67   Schweizer, *Reagan's War,* 139.

68   Ibid., 106.

69   Skinner et al., "Strategy of Campaigning," 101 (emphasis added).

objectives.[70] Still, his rhetoric in the early days of his administration was actually more nuanced, with greater emphasis on peace and avoiding the horrors of a nuclear war, than it had been earlier. Rather than continue to pursue the arms limitation efforts of the past, which he thought were both too modest and did little to prevent Soviet cheating, Reagan pushed for Strategic Arms Reduction Talks, the goal of which was to achieve substantial, verifiable reductions in weapons.[71] In November 1981, Reagan made an initial effort at arms reduction when he announced that the United States would not deploy its Pershing II tactical nuclear missiles in Europe if the Soviets would withdraw their SS-20s, SS-4s, and SS-5s, a proposal known as "Zero Option."[72] At the time, many saw the proposal as being both unbalanced and a cover for an administration that opposed real arms control. The following year, in a commencement address at Eureka College, he criticized the Soviet Union yet made clear his goal of peaceful relations. He told the graduating class that "aggressive policies [from the new Soviet leadership] will meet a firm Western response. On the other hand, a Soviet leadership devoted to improving its people's lives, rather than expanding its armed conquests, will find a sympathetic partner in the United States." Reagan then laid out a five-point policy for peace, consisting of "military balance, economic security, regional stability, arms reductions, and dialogue."[73] Clearly, in the weeks leading up to the Westminster address Reagan expressed both a strident attack on the Soviets and a hope that real arms control agreements could be achieved. As we note later, many doubted the authenticity of his commitment to arms control and feared that his aggressive policies would lead to war.

Conclusion

The period between 1945 and 1982 was an ideological journey for Ronald Reagan. It began in the late 1940s with the realization that communism posed at least as great a threat to the United States as the fascist foes of World War II had. As the

---

70   Ronald Reagan, "The President's News Conference," January 29, 1981, http://reagan.utexas.edu/archives/speeches/1981/12981b.html, 3.

71   Gaddis, *Cold War,* 225.

72   Ronald Reagan, "Remarks to Members of the National Press Club on Arms Reduction and Nuclear Weapons," November 18, 1981, http://www.reagan.utexas.edu/archives/speeches/1981/111881a.htm.

73   Ronald Reagan, "Address at Commencement Exercises at Eureka College, Eureka, Illinois," May 9, 1982, http://www.reagan.utexas.edu/archives/speeches/1982/50982a.htm, 3.

journey continued into the 1950s and 1960s, Reagan's attitudes toward the Soviet Union hardened and he began to define the conflict in moral terms, often labeling the Soviet Union as evil and rejecting any approach to foreign policy that resembled accommodation. While one might negotiate and compromise if the differences were merely political and economic, there was no room for compromise in a moral battle. Reagan was convinced that the Soviet Union eventually would be defeated, not by accommodation or by war but by the power of the democratic idea and the economic might that the idea made possible. By the 1970s and early 1980s, as Reagan made the transition from actor to governor to president, and as he moved closer to real responsibility for U.S. policy toward the Soviet Union, his views became more nuanced. While still believing communism to be an economically and morally flawed system that must be defeated, Reagan's discourse in this period began to place a greater emphasis on peace and the avoidance of nuclear war. All of these trends would be made manifest at Westminster, where they were woven together in defense of what he called the "not so fragile flower" that is democracy.

President Ronald Reagan's next four years signified a US foreign policy against the threat of Communism that would stop at nothing, no matter how much it cost the US taxpayers. On March 23, 1983, President Ronald Reagan publicly announced to the American people that he would initiate a new antiballistic nuclear program to defeat the Soviet Union, dubbed the Strategic Defense Initiative (SDI) in order to warn the Soviets that America would have another option in a nuclear war: one that did not depend solely on nuclear retaliation and to render nuclear weapons obsolete.[3] Within the Western Hemisphere, the United States would see the rise of petty Communist regimes and movements throughout Nicaragua, El Salvador, Guatemala, and Grenada. On October 23, 1983, on the Caribbean island of Grenada, the People's Revolutionary Army overthrew the legitimate government. President Reagan ordered an invasion of Grenada, dubbed Operation Urgent Fury. Over 7,000 US troops stormed ashore, the Communists were defeated in several deadly skirmishes, and months later, the United States presence departed Grenada.[4] Over the next few years, the United States doubled any spending that the Soviets planned for; furthermore, America was winning the space race, as its space shuttles were highly successful in employing spy satellites and initiating the SDI program. In June of 1987, President Ronald Reagan made a historic speech from the Brandenburg Gate in Berlin, East Germany:

> General Secretary Gorbachev, if you seek peace, if you seek prosperity for the Soviet Union and Eastern Europe, if you seek liberalization, come here to this gate.
> Mr. Gorbachev, open this gate!
> Mr. Gorbachev, tear down this wall![5]

Ultimately because of the strong character of President Reagan and his determination to combat Communists (specifically, the Soviet Union), the

---

3   SDI was a space-based missile defense program to include space-based laser systems; the system would potentially eliminate any first-strike capability of the Soviet Union. Soviet leader Mikhail Gorbachev demanded that President Reagan drop the SDI program as it would hinder the NF Treaty (Nuclear Forces Treaty) and START (Strategic Arms Reduction Talks) (US Department of State Archives, 1983).

4   According to the UN in its statement of international law, "Bearing in mind that, in accordance with Article 2, paragraph 4, of the Charter of the United Nations, all Member States are obliged to refrain in their international relations from the threat or use of force against the territorial integrity or political independence of any State or in any other manner inconsistent with the principles of the Charter (United Nations, 2013)."

5   Speech given at the Brandenburg Gate (Robinson, 2007).

dissolution of the Soviet Union occurred rapidly with the collapse of the Berlin Wall in November 1989 and the breakup of Communist countries throughout Eastern Europe. The new president George H.W. Bush initiated talks between Mikhail Gorbachev to continue the reduction of nuclear arms and help the former Soviet Union ease into democracy. Gorbachev supported open elections, and Boris Yeltsin became the first president of the Russian Federation in 1991.

Chapter 5: Identify the Following Key Players and Events

- President Ronald Reagan
  - Col. Oliver North
- Mikhail Gorbachev
  - Iran-Contra Affair
- *glasnost*
  - *perestroika*
- Reykjavik, Iceland
  - SDI (Strategic Defense Initiative)
- INF Treaty
  - Berlin Wall

Discussion Questions

1. How did President Ronald Reagan's fight become a moral fight against Communism under the Soviet Union?
2. What was one important issue during the presidential primary campaign of 1976 between President Gerald Ford and Ronald Reagan?
3. What does "living in a free world" mean to Ronald Reagan?
4. To what new defense capabilities and/or programs did President Ronald Reagan commit the US government in order to fight Communism under the Soviet Union?
5. Why did President Ronald Reagan strive to have military nuclear capability over the Soviets?

Comparative Essay

Directions: Read the following passage and write an essay that compares the actions of President Ronald Reagan's administration to that of President Trump when dealing with the Russians.

The leadership of President Vladimir Putin has produced increased tensions between Russia and the United States, from US sanctions against Russia by the Obama administration to the influence Russia has had on the last 2016 US presidential election. Cyber-attacks have become the new 21st-century nuclear bomb. How would Ronald Reagan have handled someone like Vladimir Putin? Does President Trump understand the geopolitical game with Russia that President Ronald Reagan understood with the Soviet Union? President Ronald Reagan had to deal with a world that was split in half: one side was working for the cause of freedom and the other side working for state control. President Trump is dealing with a different kind of world, one that is dominated by world powers, secondary economic powers like China, France, and Germany, and nations that are infested with terrorism, poor economics, and starvation. The Russian government has taken advantage of the Crimea situation, the Syrian civil war, Afghanistan, and North Korea. President Trump has intervened in the Syrian civil war and in Afghanistan and is working with China to subdue North Korea. Has the progress for peace achieved by President Ronald Reagan and General Secretary of the Communist Party of the Soviet Union Mikhail Gorbachev reversed itself in the 21st century?

Time Line

- 1983—President Ronald Reagan publicly announces the Strategic Defense Initiative (SDI)
- 1983—US forces invade the Communist government of Grenada
- 1987—President Reagan makes a historic speech in Berlin, East Germany
- 1988—The Soviet Union withdraws its armed forces from Afghanistan
- 1989—The Soviet Union collapses, and Communist parties are dissolved in Eastern Europe
- 1991—Boris Yeltsin becomes president of the Russian Federation

Conclusion

"Nuclear War and Chess"

Since the end of the Cold War, nuclear proliferation has always been a major global concern. Rouge nations and terrorist organizations only desire to extract the elements of such devices to produce improvised renditions of the all-powerful weapon to be used on the civilized world. The real challenge in the 21st geopolitical game is to not circumvent the obvious game between the existing superpowers of the U.S., Russia, India, and China. If a superpower plays chess, then play chess not checkers. In the game of chess each piece has a value, each piece can change the dynamic of the game, each piece is respected, there is a logical order of sequence to the game, there is a realization that the game could be lost and not worth pursuing a specific strategy based upon your opponent's moves. In the game of chess there is the possibility of rapid succession of pieces, but it is not necessary because one can receive the benefits of placing certain pieces during the middle of the game where it is most desired. When playing chess, the first move should be one that takes time for your opponent to recover from, for example, setting up the *Tarrasch Defense*. Control of the middle of the chess board is important, so it is in the real world. Strategically, leaving an impression in the Middle East and Africa (specifically Egypt) will benefit the superpower that has the time and monies to invest in such regions. The benefits of controlling such outcomes in the middle of the chess board/ Middle East and Africa predictively will benefit such superpower for hundreds of years. In chess, if one can eliminate the pawns in the middle of the board, there is a chance for more freedom of movement despite the fact your opponent may control more space. Like in chess, each superpower in a dispute should not commit more than 30 moves in total with its competitor/

enemy or risk the ultimate and foreseeable destruction of its society. The following article entitled, *The Missile-Defense Mistake: Undermining Strategic Stability and the ABM Treaty* by Igor Ivanov is a good conclusion on the global challenges at the end of the Cold War that brings to life the maintenance of strategic stability.

The Roots of "Cold War" in the 21st Century

If we look at the geopolitical spectrum in the 21st century, we see two extremes unfolding: the West versus the East. Although it looks like another possible Cold War is brewing in the 21st century, it really is not. This is an old fight between the East (Russia) and the West (Britain, France, and Turkey), and the prize is Crimea. The Crimean War lasted from 1853 to 1856, with the Russians getting the short end of the stick in the Treaty of Paris. The Treaty of Paris forced the Russians to abandon their naval operations in the Black Sea and give up their influence over Wallachia and Moldavia. The current president of Russia, Vladimir Putin, has stated that he had all nuclear options open to stop the West from dominating Crimea.[1] Russia has three specific goals in Crimea[2]: (a) control the Black Sea territory, (b) defeat the Ukrainian nationalist movement in Kiev, and (c) protect the Russian citizens, the Russian Black Sea fleet, and the Soviet air bases. The US response in 2016 to the Russians in the Black Sea has been an appropriate one. The USS *Porter*, part of the United States Sixth Fleet, arrived at the Black Sea port of Varna, Bulgaria, over Moscow's objections.[3] More US naval ships have come into the Black Sea area under the new US president, Donald Trump. President Trump has also announced that American military operations in Syria will be coming to an end, operations that were clearly upsetting the Russian government, which has been backing its long-time ally, Bashar al-Assad. Diplomats from both the United States and Russia have been set to return home as negotiations over "nothing" have occurred.

The main questions are these: (a) Did the Russian government interfere with the 2016 election between Donald Trump and Hillary Clinton?

---

1   http://www.latimes.com/world/europe/la-fg-russia-putin-crimea-20150315-story.html

2   http://www.latimes.com/world/europe/la-fg-russia-putin-crimea-20150315-story.html

3   https://www.usatoday.com/story/news/2016/06/10/russia-vows-response-us-naval-ships-entry-into-black-sea/85686822/

(b) Has the United States been arming NATO members and former Soviet Warsaw Pact members with weapons to intimidate Russia? The answers to these questions are probably yes, and that Russia is justified in matching US aggression. Should we be looking more toward the motivations of the British and the French, and why they fear any Russian expansion? Or is this something deeper? Is it because of the first Crimean War, when the British and French intervened between the Ottoman Empire and the Russian Empire? Maybe even deeper than that, is the Vatican manipulating the geopolitics of Britain and France because they fear the resurgence and takeover of the Eastern Orthodox Church? It should be acknowledged that the Catholic Church, the Pope, and the Western Roman Empire were devastated that their Roman Empire fell to the barbarians in 476 A.D[4]. and that the Eastern Roman Empire (or the Byzantine Empire) refused to come to their aid and even prospered for another thousand years, until they fell to the Ottoman army. If we examine an earlier modern root of this conflict, we see Anglo-Saxon peoples, including Celts, Romans, and Normans, versus Scandinavian and Russian peoples. The Anglo-Saxons were incredibly dissatisfied with their religious beliefs and the power of monarchy, while the Russians embraced the ruling of the Tsars and their Eastern Orthodox faith.

The discontents of the Western Europeans who immigrated to America created an atmosphere that allowed for slavery, discrimination, and Red Scare paranoia. The Russian people removed all elements of monarchy, replacing it with a more socially equal Communist system that was not very appealing to the people, mainly because Moscow, ever since the Middle Ages, had always been a promoter of trade and participant in European capitalism. However, since the United States has come on the world scene, the Russians have lost that trading advantage with Europe. Hence comes the competition for Asian markets. Russia recognizes that stability and order must take priority to ensure its hold on strategic economic markets and to maintain its influence around the world. The West manages to secretly affect the world's stock prices, distribution of oil, and supply of gold; block the legitimate transactions of world banks; and place military units and equipment all over the world, not for stability purposes, but to force the Russian government to respond, with the eventual goal of bankrupting the

---

4   This is my personal opinion as the Catholic church and the Orthodox church have continuously been in competition with each other for control of certain geographic areas throughout history.

Russian economy. There are clearly two global objectives: (a) allow the US and European governments to thrive on instability, advantage, leverage, and even mercantilism, while (b) the Russians strive for stable economic freedoms, protection of their Christian religion, and control over their own hemisphere.

The Missile-Defense Mistake

Undermining Strategic Stability and the ABM Treaty

Igor Ivanov

A mong the global challenges of the twentieth century, none was more important than eliminating the danger of nuclear war. Together, Russia, the United
States, and other countries substantially minimized this threat and began the
process of limiting and reducing nuclear arsenals. This effort resulted from a universal recognition of the strategic stability concept, the cornerstone of which is the
1972 Anti-Ballistic Missile (ABM) Treaty. Strategic stability stemmed from mutual
renunciation of strategic defense systems against intercontinental ballistic missiles,
which eliminated incentives for the Soviet Union and the United States to build up
offensive nuclear capabilities. Both states switched instead to a policy of mutual
deterrence, at reduced levels of strategic armaments. In other words, the rejection
of the nuclear "shield" made the nuclear "sword" less dangerous.

With the ABM treaty as its root, a system of international accords on arms
control and disarmament sprang up in the past decades. It includes the Strategic
Arms Limitation Treaties—SALT I and SALT II—as well as the Intermediate-Range
Nuclear Forces (INF) Treaty eliminating two classes of nuclear weapons—intermediate-range and shorter-range missiles. There followed the Strategic Arms
Reductions Treaties—START I and START II—the implementation of which will
reduce nuclear warheads fourfold. Coming next is the drafting of START III to
achieve still deeper cuts in strategic offensive arms.

Inseparable from this process is the creation of global and regional regimes
of nuclear nonproliferation and the conclusion of agreements on the prohibi-
tion of nuclear tests, the elimination of chemical weapons, and the reduction
of conventional armed forces and armaments. These agreements, comprising

Igor Ivanov is Minister of Foreign Affairs of the Russian Federation.

Igor Ivanov, "The Missile-Defense Mistake: Undermining Strategic Stability and the ABM Treaty," *Foreign Affairs, vol. 79, no. 5*, pp. 15-20. Copyright © 2000 by Council on Foreign Relations, Inc. Reprinted
with permission.

the modern architecture of international security, rest on the ABM treaty. If the foundation is destroyed, this interconnected system will collapse, nullifying 30 years of efforts by the world community.

In overcoming its ideological division the world has not become more stable. The post–Cold War threats of regional conflicts, aggressive separatism, inter-ethnic strife, international terrorism, and organized crime in conditions of globalization can be effectively met only by the concerted efforts of the world community. This is attainable, however, only when international relations, first of all among the nuclear powers, become stable and predictable. By planning to deploy a national antiballistic missile system prohibited by the ABM treaty, the United States is heading in the opposite direction. This is why such plans gravely concern Russia and many other countries, including the closest allies of the United States. Since the Cold War, the United States has not contemplated an action with such far-reaching international consequences. These consequences need to be thoroughly weighed against the hoped-for advantages of a national antiballistic missile system. Is such a system worth serious deterioration in Russia-U.S. relations, global strategic stability, and, ultimately, U.S. security?

A GAME WITH NO RULES

Washington claims that an antimissile defense system will not be directed against Russia and is a defensive measure to assure U.S. national security against new, post–Cold War threats. Why, then, must the measure be categorically opposed? After all, the United States and Russia no longer consider each other adversaries, and they face virtually the same threats and challenges, including the proliferation of weapons of mass destruction and their delivery vehicles—the threat cited by Washington to justify deploying an antimissile defense system. Russia is no less interested than the United States is in finding an effective response to this challenge. But it is convinced that remedies should be sought together or, at a minimum, should not be made to the detriment of each other's interests. Globalization, of course, does not cancel the national interests of Russia or the United States, which do not always coincide. That is why Russia is searching for balanced and well-considered solutions that ensure the security of these two and other countries and international strategic stability as a whole, while preserving the impressive positive results accumulated in recent Russian-American relations.

Does there exist, in principle, the possibility of creating a national antiballistic missile system while preserving the 1972 ABM treaty as the cornerstone of strategic stability? Lifting the ban on deployment would deprive the treaty of its essence. Some compromise modification of the ABM treaty would therefore be illusory. Another crucial element of the treaty calls for continued talks on limiting strategic offensive arms. Here, too, the gutting of its essence would have a destructive domino effect for the existing system of arms control and disarmament agreements. Thus, in accordance with the statement made when START I was signed, Russia will regard the withdrawal of the United States from the ABM treaty or the treaty's substantial violation as an exceptional circumstance giving Russia the right to withdraw from START I. In effect, a similar provision was turned into law by the Russian parliament in ratifying START II. Obviously, a direct link also exists with the drafting of START III.

If the United States unilaterally withdraws from the ABM treaty, Russia will no longer be formally bound by its obligations to reduce strategic armaments, and the very process of nuclear disarmament will be inevitably terminated, if not reversed. But Russia's concerns are by no means reduced to formalities. The capability of a national antimissile defense system to undermine Russia's nuclear deterrence is not alleviated by contentions that this system will be of a "thin" or "limited" nature. It is common knowledge that global potentials are built into the architecture of any national antimissile defense system, even at initial stages. For example, a ring of ground radar stations, capable of fulfilling antimissile defense tasks, including those being deployed in the United Kingdom, Denmark, and Norway, would be able to block the trajectories of Russian ballistic missiles. Russia would be forced to respond with neutralizing measures to ensure its own security. It is admitted in the United States that even if the U.S. antimissile defense system covers the entire territory of Russia, Russia would have sufficient means to overcome it. Indeed, such possibilities do exist. This factor, among other things, has played a substantial role in the Russian parliament's decision to ratify START II. But such neutralizing measures are an unwanted option for Russia, which is focused now on solving domestic economic problems and needs a stable international situation, not a renewed arms race.

The American experts recognize that present plans to deploy a national antimissile defense represent the intitial stage only; the system will have to be further deployed and upgraded. It will acquire new infrastructure and functional tasks. So with any deployment, the genie would be out of the jar, and then it would be not the evolution of external threats but the progress of military technology in the interests of the military-industrial complex that would dictate the rules of the game—or, to be more precise, the game with no rules. The history of the Soviet-American nuclear arms race in the 1970s and 1980s is proof of this. As long as nuclear arsenals exist, Russia and the United States will not be able to do without the ABM treaty. Only on this understanding should we search for a solution to the spread of weapons of mass destruction and missile technologies.

INFLATING THE THREAT

A realistic assessment of "new missile threats" would characterize them as hypothetical and not sufficient cause for sacrificing the ABM treaty. None of the "problem" states, as they are now referred to in the West, are likely to acquire missiles capable of reaching the United States in the foreseeable future. Moreover, it is doubtful that they would consider using them against the United States, either directly or through "missile blackmail." Their missile programs respond to regional uncertainties. This is why it would be more appropriate to speak of "problem regions" where a military conflict may break out, rather than "problem states." Should there be such a crisis, its settlement would require mainly political and diplomatic efforts.

Nevertheless, the creation of a national antimissile defense system would also have negative international consequences that would destabilize not only Russia-U.S. relations but others as well. China could be expected to take countermeasures. A new nuclear arms race could be expected in South Asia and other parts of the world. Europe would be affected, too. This progression would inevitably raise the question of the future of the INF treaty.

Nuclear nonproliferation would also be dangerously harmed. At the nuclear Nonproliferation Treaty (NPT) review conference held in New York this past spring, many countries called for vigorous measures to cut nuclear weapons stockpiles as a necessary condition for strengthening the treaty. Further nuclear arms reductions will not happen without the ABM treaty, and thus the viability of the NPT itself would be threatened.

Clearly, little deterrent influence could be brought to bear on "problem" countries. Indeed, greater global and regional instability would basically encourage arms races, including the use of technologies that are still only hypothetical. For example, military experts warn of the danger of "suitcase" delivery systems for weapons of mass destruction, which can be stealthily transported to other countries without the risk of retribution for terrorists or the need to penetrate missile defenses. The creation of a national antimissile defense system not only fails to provide an effective response to missile threats but could actually create new security challenges to the United States and the world community.

A sound approach to the problem of missile proliferation starts with the recognition that it is not the cause but the effect of more serious challenges to the world community. In other words, it is necessary to treat the disease rather than its symptoms. This requires effective political and diplomatic mechanisms to govern and legally strengthen global processes that create an international atmosphere of stability and predictability. Russia and the United States must concentrate on creating such mechanisms while it is still possible to prevent and neutralize new threats.

In particular, it is important to ensure that no country feels cornered or threatened. This will only prod such a country into looking for ways to defend itself. "Problem" countries should be given a real alternative of positive engagement in global and regional security systems. Actually, this is true of all countries, not only of those the United States considers states of concern. Each should be confident that its security can be effectively ensured by political methods and rests on a solid foundation of international law. Otherwise, many countries, even the most loyal ones, will see no alternative to weapons that have the greatest deterrent potential.

Reducing missile threats requires an approach that, unlike the planned national antimissile defense system, would neither destroy the existing system of arms control agreements nor provoke offensive buildups by threatened countries. The fundamental principle must be the most active engagement of the world community in joint efforts to strengthen strategic stability.

THE ROAD AHEAD

The world community is vitally interested in further cuts in Russian and U.S. nuclear weapons. It is not coincidental that in 1999, when the problem of national missile defense was lower on the international agenda, 80 countries supported the U.N. General Assembly resolution protecting the ABM treaty. At the same time, as the NPT review conference showed, the world is closely watching Russian and U.S. nuclear disarmament.

In addition to parliamentary ratification of START II and the Comprehensive Test Ban Treaty (CTBT), Russia has assumed an active and constructive position on START III. It is prepared to agree to a ceiling of 1,500 nuclear warheads for each party instead of the 2,000–2,500 previously agreed upon. Russia has ratified agreements reached in 1997 in New York that clearly delimited the difference between strategic and nonstrategic missile defense. These agreements, if ratified by the

United States, will foster cooperative defenses against nonstrategic missiles, the threatened use of which may become relevant in the future.

Russian President Vladimir Putin's proposal to create a pan-European nonstrategic missile-defense system emerged as a logical follow-up. A number of joint steps would be required: assessment of the nature and scale of missile proliferation and possible missile threats, development of a concept of pan-European nonstrategic missile defense and a procedure for its development and deployment, and establishment of a joint early-warning center. Also part of the proposal are joint staff exercises, joint research and experiments, development of a nonstrategic missile-defense system, and creation of nonstrategic antimissile units to protect peacekeeping forces and noncombatants.

A nonstrategic antimissile system should serve the interests of all Europe, not just one alliance. An added benefit of the Russian approach is that similar multilateral systems could be created in the future in other regions. It is also important to cooperate in creating a global missile and missile-technology control system. An international meeting of experts in Moscow in March confirmed the world's positive response to this Russian initiative. The system of global control is not an attempt to replace the Missile-Technology Control Regime (MTCR). On the contrary, it will strengthen the MTCR by providing a link between its members and nonmembers.

Finally, Russia welcomes efforts to foster constructive dialogue with the countries whose developments in this area concern the United States. In particular, the initiation of such a dialogue with the Democratic People's Republic of Korea (North Korea) and, especially, the steps taken this year toward national reconciliation between the two Koreas demonstrate that political and diplomatic ways of resolving these concerns can have encouraging results. Russia has also been instrumental in this process, as demonstrated by the recent visit to the DPRK by President Putin.

Thus there is a real alternative to attempts to destroy strategic stability: a program of joint, constructive actions in the interests of Russian, US, and global security. Russia firmly believes that such a program can be implemented and that no other reasonable alternative exists.

The discussions, including bilateral meetings, between Presidents Putin and Clinton reaffirm that Russia and the United States should continue seeking mutually acceptable solutions. Despite some difficulties and disagreements, the positive development of Russia-US relations should not change. Initial steps have been taken, such as the bilateral agreement to establish in Moscow the Joint Center for the Exchange of Data from Early Warning Systems and Notification of Missile Launches. Russia believes that representatives of the European Union, China, and other countries should also be involved. More can be done jointly to prevent the proliferation of missile capabilities, including export controls on sensitive technologies. Finally, not only the parties but the entire world will benefit from Russia-U.S. cooperation on nonstrategic missile defense systems. Regional systems could be created with the participation of all interested countries that abide by the NPT and the CTBT.

The maintenance of strategic stability is not a one-time action. It requires constant attention from the world community and leadership from Russia and the United States. The importance of strategic stability for international security is so great that it must not be made subject to politics, domestic considerations, or unilateral foreign policy. This is the only way to ensure stability, prosperity, and a democratic world order in the twenty-first century.

Bibliography

Alien Registration Act of 1940. (n.d.). Retrieved from The University of Tennessee: http://web.utk.edu/~scheb/library/smithact.htm

Belasco, A., et al. (2007). *Congressional Restrictions on U.S. Military Operations in Vietnam, Cambodia, Laos, Somalia, and Kosovo: Funding and Non-Funding Approaches*. Retrieved from CRS Report for Congress: https://fas.org/sgp/crs/natsec/RL33803.pdf

C-Span Archives. (n.d.). Retrieved from President Eisenhower 1953 Inaugural Address: https://www.youtube.com/watch?v=SwenOlpbvTA

Central Intelligence Agency. (1963). *Khruschev's role in the current controversy over Soviet defense policy*. Retrieved from Central Intelligence Agency: https://www.cia.gov/library/readingroom/docs/caesar-33.pdf

Chicago Tribune. (1965). Retrieved from Chicago Tribune: http://archives.chicagotribune.com/1965/03/08/page/1/article/shoot-back-if-fired-upon-troops-told

Declassification, C. o. (1946). *Statement of recomendations on release of atom bomb project information*. Retrieved from Truman Library: https://trumanlibrary.org/whistlestop/study_collections/bomb/large/documents/pdfs/34.pdf

Dennis v. United States, 341 U.S. 494 (U.S. Supreme Court June 4, 1951).

Harry S. Truman Library and Museum. (n.d.). *Background Essay: The Mashall Plan and the Cold War*. Retrieved from Harry S. Truman Library and Museum: https://www.trumanlibrary.org/dbq/docs/marshallplan/MarshallPlan_Handouts.pdf

Jimmy Carter Sate of the Union. (1980). Retrieved from Jimmy Carter Presidentila Museum: https://www.jimmycarterlibrary.gov/documents/speeches/su80jec.phtml

John F. Kennedy Presidential Library and Museum. (2017). *Americans in Space*. Retrieved from John F. Kennedy Presidential Libary and Museum: https://www.jfklibrary.org/Education/Students/Americans-in-Space.aspx

Kifner, J. (1996). *McGeorge Bundy Dies at 77; Top Adviser in Vietnam Era*. Retrieved from The New York Times: http://www.nytimes.com/1996/09/17/us/mcgeorge-bundy-dies-at-77-top-adviser-in-vietnam-era.html

Lei, X. (2014, April). *China as a Permanent Member of the United Nations Security Council*. Retrieved from Freidrich, Ebert, and Stiftung: http://library.fes.de/pdf-files/iez/10740.pdf

Mashall, G. C. (1947). Retrieved from Harvard University Library: http://library.harvard.edu/sites/default/files/1947_marshall.pdf

NASA. (n.d.). *SP-4105 The Birth of NASA*. Retrieved from NASA: https://history.nasa.gov/SP-4105/ch6.htm

NATO. (1949, April 4). Retrieved from North Atlantic Treaty Organization: http://www.nato.int/cps/en/natolive/official_texts_17120.htm

Presidential Debate in Cleveland. (1980). Retrieved from The American Presidency Project: http://www.presidency.ucsb.edu/ws/index.php?pid=29408

Reagan Foundation. (n.d.). *From the archives Reagan, Hollywood and the Red Scare*. Retrieved from Reagan Foundation: https://www.reaganfoundation.org/media/51313/red-scare.pdf

Richard Nixon Foundation. (2017). *10 things you need to know about Nixon the Congressman*. Retrieved from Richard Nixon Foundation: https://www.nixonfoundation.org/2016/05/10-things-you-need-to-know-about-nixon-the-congressman/

Robinson, P. (2007, Summer). *"Tear down this wall" How Top Advisers Opposed Reagan's Challenge to Gorbachev—But Lost*. Retrieved from National Archives: https://www.archives.gov/publications/prologue/2007/summer/berlin.html

Semenov, N. N. (1946). *Some problems relating to chain reactions and the theory of combustion*. Retrieved from Nobel Prize: http://www.nobelprize.org/nobel_prizes/chemistry/laureates/1956/semenov-lecture.pdf

The Real News. (2017). Retrieved from The Real News: http://therealnews.com/t2/

Truman, H. S. (1947). *Special Message to the Congress on Greece and Turkey: The Truman Doctrine*. Retrieved from Harry S. Truman Library & Museum: https://trumanlibrary.org/publicpapers/index.php?pid=2189&st=&st1

Universal Newsreel Outtakes. (2016). Retrieved from Universal Newsreel Outtakes: https://www.bing.com/videos/search?q=Richard+Nixon+holding+micro+-film+HUAC&view=detail&mid=8E528B73B33428B1A5DD8E528B73B-33428B1A5DD&FORM=VIRE

US Department of State.(1983). *Strategic Defense Initiative*. Retrieved from U.S. Department of States Archives: https://2001-2009.state.gov/r/pa/ho/time/rd/104253.htm

US Department of State. (n.d.). *The Berlin Airlift, 1948–1949*. Retrieved from U.S. Department of the State, Office of the Historian, Bureau of Public Affairs: https://history.state.gov/milestones/1945-1952/berlin-airlift

US Department of State.(n.d.). *The Eisenhower Doctrine, 1957*. Retrieved from U.S. Department of State, Office of the Historian, Bureau of Public Affairs: https://history.state.gov/milestones/1953-1960/eisenhower-doctrine

US Secretary of State. (2017). *Rapprochement with China, 1972*. Retrieved from U.S. Secretary of State Office of the Historian: https://history.state.gov/milestones/1969-1976/rapprochement-china

United Nations General Assembly. (1983). *The situation in Grenada*. New York: Uniated Nations.

White, J. (2016). *Cold War International History Conference: Paper by John White*. Retrieved from National Archives: https://www.archives.gov/research/foreign-policy/cold-war/conference/white.html

Yates v. United Sates (U.S. Supreme Court June 17, 1957).

Me, Again

Rediscovering worth, Renewing faith, Reclaiming hope

Adrienne Forehand

Me, Again